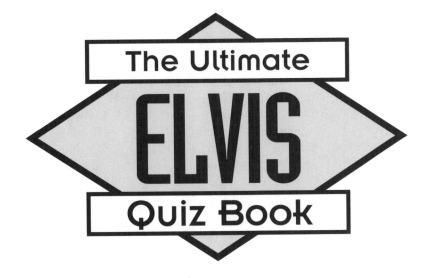

The Ultimate
ELVIS
Quiz Book

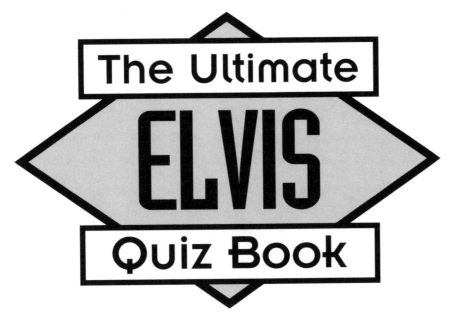

The Ultimate ELVIS Quiz Book

What Do You Know About the King of Rock & Roll?

W. KENT MOORE and **DAVID L. SCOTT**

RUTLEDGE HILL PRESS®
Nashville, Tennessee

Copyright © 1991, 1999 by W. Kent Moore and David L. Scott.

Photograph on page 90 courtesy of the National Archives. Photograph on page 101 courtesy of the Memphis Convention and Visitors Bureau. All other photographs are courtesy of Wide World Photos.

Published in Nashville, Tennessee, by Rutledge Hill Press, Inc., 211 Seventh Avenue North, Nashville, Tennessee 37219. Distributed in Canada by H. B. Fenn & Company, Ltd., 34 Nixon Road, Bolton, Ontario, L7E 1W2. Distributed in Australia by The Five Mile Press Pty., Ltd., 22 Summit Road, Noble Park, Victoria 3174. Distributed in New Zealand by Tandem Press, 2 Rugby Road, Birkenhead, Auckland 10. Distributed in the United Kingdom by Verulam Publishing, Ltd., 152a Park Street Lane, Park Street, St. Albans, Hertfordshire AL2 2AU.

Typesetting by E. T. Lowe, Nashville, Tennessee

Text design by Bateman Design.

ISBN 1-55853-748-1

Printed in the United States of America

1 2 3 4 5 6 7 8 9 — 04 03 02 01 00 99

To the many Elvis fans
who have helped to keep his music alive

CONTENTS

Quizzes

A Note to Our Fellow Elvis Fans

First of all, we want you to know how much we appreciate your making the decision to buy this book. We put in many enjoyable hours working on the manuscript, and it gives us a great deal of satisfaction to know that you will be sharing the result of these hours with us.

More than just another book about Elvis, *The Ultimate Elvis Quiz Book* is designed to get you actively involved in remembering the King as you attempt to work the various quizzes and puzzles. Many of you out there may consider yourselves to be experts on Elvis. Well, here's your chance to prove it! The questions vary in difficulty; some are easy, but we believe many of them will challenge even the most devoted fan. Even if you can't answer all of the questions in this book, take heart. By reading the answers provided at the back, you can learn many *new* tidbits of information about the man who forever changed the face of rock & roll.

The Ultimate Elvis Quiz Book contains more than one thousand questions to test your knowledge about Elvis Presley. The quizzes have a variety of formats, including word scrambles, crossword puzzles, fill-in-the-blanks, multiple-choice questions, and write-in answers. The quizzes cover topics such as people, dates, and events pertaining to Elvis's life, items about his movies, and, of course, his music. We hope that the quizzes will be both interesting and informative and that *The Ultimate Elvis Quiz Book* will give you and your friends many hours of pleasure.

Acknowledgments

Although these books are listed in the Bibliography at the back of this book, we would like to make special note of three sources that proved to be extremely helpful to us. We highly recommend all three books to Elvis fans.

1. *The Billboard Book of Top 40 Hits* by Joel Whitburn was an invaluable source of information with regard to chart positions and dates for Elvis hits. In our opinion, Joel Whitburn has the best job in America.

2. *Elvis: His Life from A to Z* by Fred L. Worth and Steve D. Tamerius is a true encyclopedia of information about Elvis's music and personal life. This is a must-have.

3. *The Boy Who Dared to Rock: The Definitive Elvis* by Paul Lichter was especially helpful with regard to recording sessions information, including information on songs, dates, and backup groups.

Introduction

Although other entertainers, such as Bill Haley, Chuck Berry, Jerry Lee Lewis, and Carl Perkins, all had important pioneering influences on early rock music, it was Elvis who had the ability, magnetism, popularity, and lasting power to ensure that rock & roll would always be an important part of the pop music landscape. As all true Elvis fans know, however, Elvis Presley was not just a rock singer. In fact, much of his appeal and impact was due to his amazing versatility. During his childhood, Elvis was greatly influenced by gospel music and by rhythm & blues. He combined aspects of gospel, R&B, and country to develop a style all his own. Few other artists, if any, can perform all these varieties of music: spunky rock songs like "Hard Headed Woman" and "Jailhouse Rock," lighter pop songs like "Return to Sender" and "Good Luck Charm," country classics like "I'm So Lonesome I Could Cry" and "Help Me Make It Through the Night," blues songs like "Blue Christmas" and "A Mess of Blues," middle-of-the-road standards like "My Way" and "What Now My Love," sensitive ballads like "Can't Help Falling in Love" and "It's Now or Never," and religious songs like "How Great Thou Art" and "Crying in the Chapel."

Actually, Elvis is more than the King of Rock & Roll; he is a cultural phenomenon who has affected our entire society. It has been more than twenty years since Elvis died; yet his popularity is still very much alive. Each year millions of dollars' of Elvis products continue to sell. Clearly, interest in his music and life is still strong.

As you read this book, let your thoughts drift back to those heady days of the 1950s when rock & roll was being molded by such giants as Little Richard, Buddy Holly, and, of course, Elvis, or to the early 1960s when rock & roll was being further refined by Ricky Nelson, the Everly Brothers, Roy Orbison, Brook Benton, Connie Francis, and Elvis again. Remember what it was like back then when your parents were convinced that these musicians and their music were passing fads. Remember how these singers dressed, how they styled their hair, and how they sang their hearts out to us. Were you going steady when Elvis sang "Wear My Ring Around Your Neck" or experiencing another romantic disappointment when Connie Francis pleaded "Don't Break the Heart That Loves You"?

We tend to remember what we were doing when certain songs were popular, especially during our adolescence. Perhaps these singers and their songs help to keep us forever young. So remember those past days and especially remember Elvis.

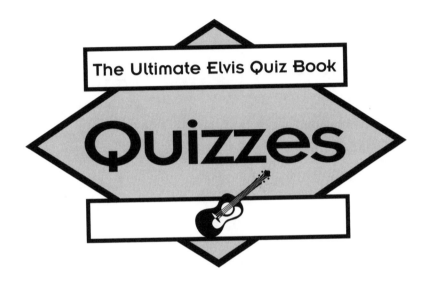

The Ultimate Elvis Quiz Book

Quizzes

Takin' It Easy with Elvis

Here is a relatively easy warm-up quiz to warm you up to Elvis. There are no fancy crosswords or matching items here. Just answer the questions and get ready for the bigger brainteasers that come later.

1. In an early fifties hit, what didn't Elvis want stepped on?

2. What was Elvis's first two-sided Top Ten single? Name both sides.

3. What was Elvis's first movie?

4. In what country did Elvis meet his future wife?

5. What did Elvis give away during concerts?

6. What was the Colonel's full name?

7. What was Elvis's favorite soft drink?

8. What was Elvis's 1973 worldwide TV special called?

9. In what town did Elvis die?

10. What was Elvis's wife's name?

11. With what company did Elvis record during most of his career?

12. On what well-known southern radio show was Elvis heard several times in the mid-1950s?

13. What vocal group is most closely associated with Elvis's early recordings?

14. What was Elvis's last Top Ten single?

15. What early hit inspired hundreds of fans to send Elvis stuffed animals?

16. What was Elvis's middle name? (Spell it correctly.)

17. What is the name of Elvis's Memphis mansion?

18. In what town did Elvis attend junior high school?

19. What was Elvis's father's first name?

20. What was the name of Elvis's customized Convair jet?

2

21. In what Las Vegas hotel did Elvis perform during the late 1960s and the 1970s? (The hotel changed names in 1971. For extra credit, give both names.)

   _____

22. On what Memphis street is Elvis's home located?   _____

23. Not counting documentaries, what was Elvis's last movie?   _____

★ **In 1972 Elvis became the first solo performer to sell out Madison Square Garden for four straight shows.**

A young Elvis between takes at a 1956 Nashville recording session for RCA.

Elvis as a guest on the "Steve Allen Show" in 1956 with Imogene Coca and the host.

Elvis Is Number One

The titles to each of Elvis's eighteen number-one songs are hidden below. In order to complete this quiz, you not only have to know the names of the songs, you also have to locate the titles. Here's a hint: Only one title is listed diagonally and no title is displayed backward.

```
I L O V E L V I S N E E L S W H I A B L T D E A
A W N E B E D A V I D A N D K A Y G O A N T E N
N H A R D H E A D E D W O M A N N T R S U R R E
I B I N T N B R T R N T H R L E A E N U A N D I
R U N T T F U E N I T A N D L O Y O R R B I G E
B I N G C Y G Y T T I N R O S U R R E N D E R N
A J A I L G O O D L U C K C H A R M E E O I T E
W S E R C H U U C E A M H E O R A R T N N T J M
J U R R S U S L I C I O U S O I N D S D T S A T
G S G R E T H O U N D D O G K A D N L Y O N I L
S P I L N O W N E S E T A B U P A R S S T U L N
D I D O N T B E C R U E L U P K A Y T V A L H O
B C O V D A V S H O O D D D A V I D U C N O O E
E I N E K A Y O A R T D O Y S T E V C L O W U S
T O O M U C H M S H E Y B E O O K A K I A M S E
A U N E K A Y E E L A B I G H U N K O L O V E Y
O S E T N O W T V I S E R U S H I O N S H E R W
I M O E V I C O T O W A L O W N D L Y M I T O C
T I T N I T S N O W O R N E V E R O O N I T C L
O N E D E L V I S I S K I N G Y E P U V E P K N
I D N E D I G G G V A L D O S T A G A A E E L N
O S T R K E Y H R U S H V I L L E I N D N Y T R
G A A H E A R T B R E A K H O T E L I N T H O U
N A B D E A R E L V I S I S A L I V E N O W H U
```

5

★ Titles and Subtitles

Many of the songs recorded by Elvis had subtitles in addition to the main titles. For example, on the Clambake *album, there is a song titled "How Can You Lose" with a subtitle "(What You Never Had)." For the song titles below, probe the subtitle zone of your brain and then fill in the subtitles in the parentheses.*

1. "Anyway You Want Me (_____)"

2. "(_____) Teddy Bear"

3. "Don't Be Cruel (_____)"

4. "(_____) A Fool Such as I"

5. "It Is No Secret (_____)"

6. "(_____) Devil in Disguise"

7. "Without Love (_____)"

8. "Release Me (_____)"

9. "If You Love Me (_____)"

10. "Long Legged Girl (_____)"

11. "(_____) His Latest Flame"

12. "(_____) Baby, I Don't Care"

13. "I'll Hold You in My Heart (_____)"

14. "Santa Bring My Baby Back (_____)"

★ **Elvis's first Grammy nomination was for "A Fool Such as I" in the category Record of the Year. The year was 1959 and the song didn't win.**

B Sides of Singles

Elvis recorded twenty-eight singles in which both the A and the B sides reached the Top Forty. (For our purposes, the B side is the side that ranked lower on Billboard's charts.) Listed below are fourteen of these B sides. See if you are able to name the A side of each record.

1. "I Was the One" _____

2. "Ain't That Loving You, Baby" _____

3. "Hound Dog" _____

4. "Viva Las Vegas" _____

5. "Rags to Riches" _____

6. "I Got Stung" _____

7. "Rock-a-Hula Baby" _____

8. "Fame and Fortune" _____

9. "Loving You" _____

10. "Witchcraft" _____

11. "Wild in the Country" _____

12. "Anyway You Want Me" _____

13. "The Next Step Is Love" _____

14. "A Mess of Blues" _____

Bonus Question: For one of the singles listed above, both sides reached number one. Which single was it, and how was that possible?

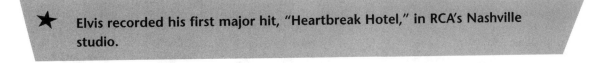

★ **Elvis recorded his first major hit, "Heartbreak Hotel," in RCA's Nashville studio.**

The Puzzling King

The King of Rock & Roll may have been puzzling to the uninformed, but real Elvis fans could see that he cut through to the heart of rock & roll like nobody else. See if you can work through this crossword puzzle that deals with a wide range of matters that were relevant to Elvis's life.

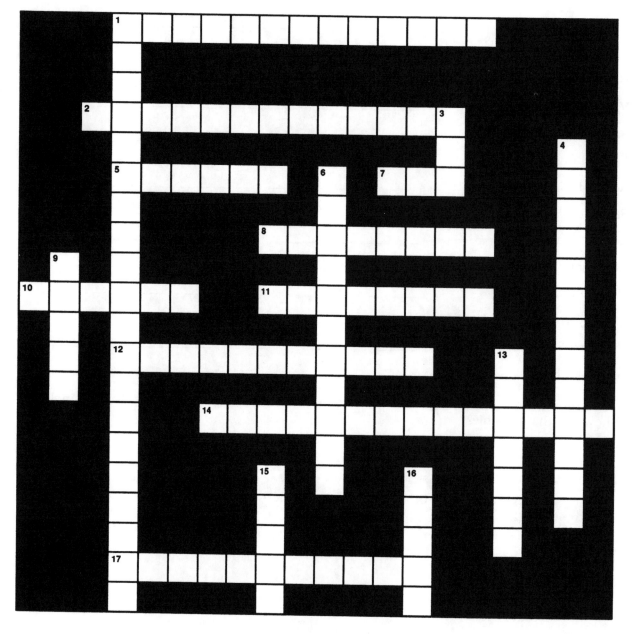

ACROSS

1. First Elvis recording played on the air
2. Miss Tennessee girlfriend of Elvis
5. Elvis's mother
7. Elvis's first recording label
8. Wrote "In the Ghetto"
10. Elvis was born here
11. Leader of the Stamps Quartet
12. "Last Date" pianist who plays on some Elvis recordings
14. Played Elvis's mother in *Blue Hawaii*
17. Elvis's record producer at start of his career

DOWN

1. Meaning of TCB
3. Mary Tyler Moore role in *Change of Habit*
4. Elvis's third movie
6. Minister stepbrother of Elvis
9. Elvis's high school
13. Elvis's manager before the Colonel
15. First name of "Kentucky Rain" songwriter
16. Elvis's stillborn twin

Elvis takes his Army pre-induction test in 1957.

★ After singing on "The Grand Ole Opry," Elvis was told by a talent coordinator that he should go back to driving a truck.

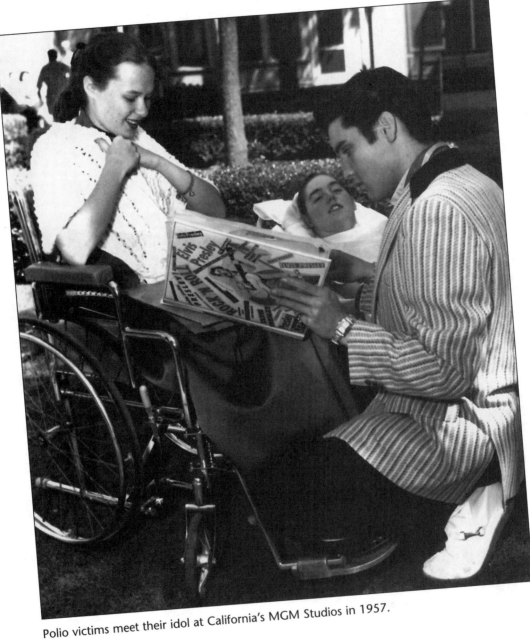

Polio victims meet their idol at California's MGM Studios in 1957.

★ Reportedly, Elvis felt somewhat embarrassed about being called the King. He thought the designation should be reserved for Jesus, the King of Kings.

Not So High, But Great Anyway

Although it may seem as if all of Elvis's records made it into the Top Ten, some of his finest songs languished well below that elite level. See if you are able to unscramble the titles from the following selections that made the Top One Hundred but never cracked the Top Forty. Be warned that the words as well as the letters of each word are scrambled.

1. TI CAKB GRNIGIBN
   _____

2. DASEIR KRCO NO
   _____

3. 'INNRRBBEEKCU
   _____

4. NICMREAA NA IGYOLTR
   _____

5. OERSS EILDK AAMM EHT
   _____

6. LNYO 'SIT OLVE
   _____

7. LEEEBIV LONY
   _____

8. FO EARC KAET ERH ODGO
   _____

9. ETH THARE RFO
   _____

10. OD OUY EMCO MFOR EHERW
    _____

11. SOURYFLE TLE OG
    _____

12. TI OS ELESF HGRIT
    _____

13. LOUYL' NEOAL REEVN LAKW
    _____

14. EM RETHSE' WSYLAA
    _____

15. 'OL KAES RFO SIETM
    _____

★ **Elvis gave Tom Jones, whom he considered both a friend and a competitor, one of his famous TCB medallions.**

11

Elvis shows a girlfriend his Graceland estate in 1957.

★ **Elvis appeared only once on "The Grand Ole Opry." The date was October 2, 1954.**

Identify the Year

For an incredible twenty-two consecutive years, from 1956 through 1977, Elvis had at least one single that made the Top Forty. One single from each of those years is listed below. Give the correct year for each of the songs listed.

1. _____ "Burning Love"

2. _____ "Crying in the Chapel"

3. _____ "Devil in Disguise"

4. _____ "A Fool Such as I"

5. _____ "Hurt"

6. _____ "I Really Don't Want to Know"

7. _____ "I Want You, I Need You, I Love You"

8. _____ "In the Ghetto"

9. _____ "Indescribably Blue"

10. _____ "Kissin' Cousins"

11. _____ "Little Sister"

12. _____ "Love Letters"

13. _____ "My Boy"

14. _____ "One Night"

15. _____ "Promised Land"

16. _____ "She's Not You"

17. _____ "Steamroller Blues"

18. _____ "Stuck on You"

19. _____ "Too Much"

20. _____ "U.S. Male"

21. _____ "Way Down"

22. _____ "The Wonder of You"

★

Elvis's first Grammy Award came in 1967 in the category Best Sacred Performance for his *How Great Thou Art* album. The album has been a steady seller over the years and was certified as a double-platinum record, which is unusual for a religious album.

⭐ 8 Where on Earth Was Elvis?

Even though Elvis avoided travel outside the United States (he did play a few concerts in Canada and, of course, was stationed in West Germany while in the army), various locations visited by the King hold special memories for his fans. See how you do with the following questions that relate to special places in Elvis's life. In each case, name the city.

1. Where was Elvis's last live concert? _____

2. Where was the King married? _____

3. Where was Elvis's first concert following his 1969–70 Las Vegas comeback? _____

4. Where was Elvis's ranch, the Circle G, located? _____

5. Where was the King's first live concert? _____

6. Where was Elvis and Priscilla's first home following their marriage? _____

7. Where did Vernon Presley's second marriage take place? _____

8. Where did *Jailhouse Rock* premiere? _____

9. Where did the "Welcome Home, Elvis" television show, made after Elvis's army discharge, take place? _____

10. Where did *Love Me Tender* premiere? _____

11. What was the location of the first canceled concert following Elvis's death? _____

12. Where was Elvis's first concert outside the United States? _____

⭐ Graceland was first opened to the public on June 7, 1982.

⭐ The recording of "Softly, as I Leave You," which was released after Elvis's death, was taken from a tape made on a private tape recorder during one of his Las Vegas concerts.

Let's Go to the Movies

Elvis made thirty-three movies during his career. Although the films were not always widely acclaimed by the critics, a true Elvis fan should, at the very least, know the title of each film. Find the fourteen Elvis movie titles hidden in the puzzle below.

```
D S Y Z F P D B E M L S U Y Z J X A Q E S T A Z X
O P R X G L W O D Q F O B O O V I Q O B U R O J O
C X J I V K P P Y M O Z V Y R N B J G O P S E N J
N F A X K D Q Q W O O P Y I Y X Y R B L I T E C O
D X C K A S R U J U H G C D N A O A R I T L V L T
R R J H W F O G X A J D U X W G T A N R B S C A X
N W K O A D U W B Y I J I A Q S Y G J U F M B M F
N A B K N H A C J L J L Y F U W V O O K Y Q Y B I
W Y L I C V B X Z X Z A H O M E T R U H J Z G A I
R S U M A C C F U V T X R O F W T K P Z E B X K Y
Q E E D I L D R O S J T M D U E E R Q L M J L E K
S O H E W B X D S E P L X A L S Y U O R M U U Q N
S A A B X R V A F B O O E B Z Z E E H R X Z N K J
H A W O G W J D U J L D U H E Z R R B H F J L K L
X T A R C N D Y D B T O B P I C U E O Q Z W D X O
M I I A M J T J S H D B U I G A I S Y C V W F Z H
J G I H O I N N P B S B C N L D Q A X Q K L C Q Q
W G I R L S G I R L S G I R L S W E C F H Q W C E
U R C R G P A Y L J X K R W F D Y B E K E R V M L
S L D I L C F C H C H A N G E O F H A B I T E L O
R N I A Y H C U L O V E M E T E N D E R S L I Q L
M R S T Y Z A K L M S V P J I U A H Q H K B B K Q
K Z N M T X R P I H T S K P I S V D J C G D B P V
E M V A Z L V I P J I H Y D D S W P I I X E M Q L
N Z P W Y C U F C Y L A W P Q K I T Z P Y J N T G
```

★ **Elvis did not receive top billing in *Love Me Tender*, his first film. He was listed third, below Richard Egan and Debra Paget.**

15

A Whole Lotta Blues Goin' On

Elvis recorded at least fourteen songs that contain the word blue *or* blues *in the title. Try to finish the title of each of the following songs. A small hint is given about each song.*

1. "Blue _ _ _ _ _ _ _ _ _ _ _"   Recorded by Carl Perkins

2. "_ _ _ _ _ _ _ _ _ _ _ Blues"   Recorded by Roy Orbison

3. "_ _ _ _ _ _ _ _ _ _ _ _ _ _ Blue"   Sad ballad from 1967

4. "_ _ _ _ _ _ _ _ _ _ Blue"   Often used at weddings

5. "Blue _ _ _ _ _ _ _"   Most popular movie LP

6. "Blue _ _ _ _ _ _ _ _ _ _"   Seasonal standard

7. "_ _ _ _ _ _ _ _ Blues"   Flip side of "It's Now or Never"

8. "Blue _ _ _ _ _ _ _ _ _ _ _ _ _ _"   A popular bluegrass song

9. "_. _. Blues"   A movie (easy question)

10. "_ _ _ _ _ _ _ _ _ Blues"   Sung in a movie when Elvis was in jail

11. "Blue _ _ _ _"   Number-one record for the Marcels

12. "_ _ _ _ _ Blue"   Single released shortly before Elvis's death

13. "_ _ _ _ _ _ _ _ Blues _ _ _ _ _ _"   An early Sun recording

---

★ Roy Orbison went by Graceland to offer his song "Only the Lonely" to Elvis, but Elvis was asleep at the time. Thus, the opportunity opened up for the man with the dark glasses.

14. "_ _ _ _ _   _ _   Blue   _ _ _ _ _

   _ _ _ _ _   _ _   _ _ _ _   _ _ _ _ _"

An up-tempo country song from Elvis's second RCA album

15. "Blue   _ _ _ _ _"

Flip side of "Tell Me Why"

16. "_ _ _ _ _ _ _ _ _ _ _ _   Blues"

Single taken from *Elvis: Aloha from Hawaii*

Bonus Question 1: What Fats Domino hit containing *blue* in the title was also recorded by Elvis? (Is this easy or what?)

Bonus Question 2 (a much more difficult question): Which two Elvis LPs contain the Fats Domino hit?

A monogrammed Elvis with a female companion in 1957 following a private showing of *Loving You*.

A Crossword for the King's Movies

Although some critics cast disparaging remarks at many of Elvis's movies, the faithful continued to flood past the ticket counters to see the King on the big screen. After all, where else could you experience light-hearted fun and, at the same time, hear great songs such as "Return to Sender" (Girls! Girls! Girls!), "Jailhouse Rock" (Jailhouse Rock), and "Can't Help Falling in Love" (Blue Hawaii)? True Elvis fans will be able to breeze through most of this puzzle.

ACROSS

4. Elvis's last regular movie
5. Person who appeared most frequently as the female lead opposite Elvis (first name)
7. Person (besides Elvis) who appeared in the most Elvis movies
10. Movie in which Vernon Presley made his acting debut
11. The *Mississippi* _____ (riverboat in *Frankie and Johnny*)
12. Hollywood veteran who produced the most Elvis movies
13. Location of the World's Fair in *It Happened at the World's Fair*
14. Star of "I Led Three Lives," whose last movie was *Change of Habit* (last name)
15. Later TV name of the actress who played a nun in *Change of Habit*
16. Nightclub in which Elvis sang "The Love Machine" in *Easy Come, Easy Go*

DOWN

1. Played opposite Elvis in the King's first movie (last name)
2. Type of poster on which Elvis's picture (as Jesse Wade) appeared in *Charro!*
3. Backup group that appeared in *King Creole*
5. Nancy Sinatra's solo in *Speedway* was "Your Groovy _____"
6. Last name of a president's daughter in *Kissin' Cousins*
8. Sexy actress who made her screen debut in *Roustabout*
9. Adopted daughter of this film star made her movie debut in *Wild in the Country*
14. Movie in which Elvis wore a beard

★ Elvis's last movie, *Elvis on Tour*, was voted the Best Documentary of 1972 by the Hollywood Foreign Press Association.

★ Elvis's mother and many of his fans were upset when Elvis's character died in *Love Me Tender*. He was not shown dying in any subsequent movie roles.

★12 Second to Elvis

Many songs only made it to number two on the charts because Elvis already had a song that was number one at the time. Listed below on the right are six songs that were "second to Elvis" and on the left are the six Elvis songs that beat them out. Match each number-two song with the Elvis song that was number one at the same time.

_____ 1. "Hard Headed Woman"

_____ 2. "Teddy Bear"

_____ 3. "Are You Lonesome Tonight?"

_____ 4. "All Shook Up"

_____ 5. "Heartbreak Hotel"

_____ 6. "Stuck on You"

A. "Greenfields"

B. "Little Darlin' "

C. "Bye Bye Love"

D. "Last Date"

E. "Hot Diggity"

F. "Yakety Yak"

Bonus Question: Name the artist who recorded each number-two song and the year in which each of these number-one/number-two pairings occurred.

Elvis and his teddy bear, ready for Christmas at home.

In Love with Elvis

Elvis recorded approximately fifty songs that contain the words love, loving, *or* lovin'. *A few of them, such as "Love Me Tender," "Love Me," and "Loving You," are obvious. Try your hand at using the clues to complete the titles of these songs.*

1. "_ _ _ _ _ _ _ Love"   A hit song for Tom Jones

2. "_ _ _ _ _ Love   An Olivia Newton-John hit
   _ _ (_ _ _ _ _ _ _ _ _)"

3. "_ _ _ _ _ _ _ _ _ _ _ Love"   Recorded by Johnny Ace

4. "_ _ _ _ _ _ Love"   A Bob Wills tune

5. "_ _ _ _ _ _ _ _ Loving   The flip side of "Ask Me"
   _ _ _ _ _ _ _"

6. "_ _ _ _ _ _ _ Love"   A gold record in 1972

7. "_ _ _ _ _ _ _ _ _ _   Written by Don Gibson
   Loving _ _ _"

8. "_ _ _ _ _ _ _ _ _ _ _ _   From the movie *G.I. Blues*
   _ _ _ _ _ _ _ _ Love"

9. "_ _ _ _ _ _ _ _ _ _ _ _ _   A big hit for the Righteous Brothers
   Lovin' _ _ _ _ _ _ _"

10. "_ _ _ _ _ _ _ _ _ _   From the movie *Frankie and Johnny*
    _ _ _ _ Loving _ _"

11. "_ _ _ _ _ _ _ _ _ _ _   Flip side of "I've Lost You"
    _ _ Love"

12. "_ _ _ Lovin' _ _"   Recorded by Peter, Paul and Mary

21

★ 14 Musical Roots and Influences

Elvis became interested in music at an early age and especially enjoyed listening to southern gospel music and spirituals, rhythm & blues, and country music. He blended these various styles of music into a unique sound that changed the course of American popular music. Below are descriptions of twenty-two singers whom Elvis enjoyed or was influenced by. Unscramble their names.

1. Pioneer country singer known as the Singing Brakeman.

   DRRSOEG MEJMII

   _____

2. Blues singer whom Elvis heard on Beale Street in Memphis while still in school. (The initials make this easy, but the man is too important to omit.)

   NIGK B B

   _____

3. Two early Elvis songs—"That's All Right (Mama)" and "My Baby Left Me"—were originally written and recorded by this man.

   UHRRAT DPUCUR

   _____

4. Elvis may have borrowed his gospel singing style from this artist.

   KAEJ SEHS

   _____

5. Nickname of blues artist who recorded "Hound Dog" before Elvis.

   AMAM NRTTNOOH GBI

   _____

6. Perhaps Elvis's favorite singer.

   NAMRIT AEND

   _____

7. Country artist known as the Singing Ranger who had his biggest hits in the 1950s and who appeared with Elvis on "The Grand Ole Opry."

   NWOS KAHN

   _____

8. Black gospel group that influenced both Elvis and the Jordanaires. Elvis recorded several of this group's songs.

   TAEG TUTERQA EDNGLO

9. A black singer who sang "Lonely Teardrops" and was one of Elvis's favorite artists.

   OILSNW EJKCAI

   _____

22

10. Popular country artist of the 1940s and 1950s. Elvis recorded several of his hits, including "Peace in the Valley." His music is more closely related to that of Pat Boone than to that of Elvis.

LYFEO DER

_____

11. Elvis enjoyed this easy-listening black quartet that recorded "That's When Your Heartaches Begin."

KNI TPSSO

_____

12. Rhythm & blues singer who recorded "Mystery Train."

NROIUJ TILETL EKRPRA

_____

13. Country singer with a velvet voice who appeared with Elvis on "The Louisiana Hayride."

VSREEE MJI

_____

14. Elvis admired the vocal ability of this black singer, who recorded "Unchained Melody" long before Elvis.

YRO MLHNOTIA

_____

15. The Father of Bluegrass, who wrote and recorded "Blue Moon of Kentucky."

LIBL NREOMO

_____

16. Elvis called him "the greatest singer in the world." His 1963 version of "Mean Woman Blues" had different lyrics than the version Elvis sang in *Loving You.*

SRBINOO YRO

_____

17. Known as the Texas Troubadour, this member of the Country Music Hall of Fame had Elvis on his "Midnight Jamboree" radio program.

BTBU SNRETE

_____

18. This country music giant wrote and sang many big hits, including "I'm So Lonesome I Could Cry," which Elvis sang in his *Aloha from Hawaii* concert.

MLIIWSLA KNHA

_____

19. A black singer from the early fifties whose music never dented the Top Forty but was a major influence on Elvis's pop ballads.

LIYBL TENEKCSI

_____

20. He composed and originally recorded "Good Rockin' Tonight" and was known as a black singer with a white sound. (Sort of the opposite of Elvis, perhaps.)

YOR NRBWO

_____

(continued on the following page)

21. Rhythm & blues singer who recorded "Tiger Man" for Sun Records in the early 1950s.

AMOHTS FSUUR

_____

22. Mississippi blues singer who wrote and recorded "Got My Mojo Working" in the mid-fifties.

DUYMD ASRWET

_____

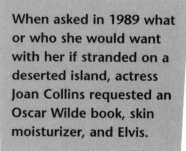

★

When asked in 1989 what or who she would want with her if stranded on a deserted island, actress Joan Collins requested an Oscar Wilde book, skin moisturizer, and Elvis.

In 1957, a nonplussed Elvis learns of a 60-day draft delay while Miss Ohio and Miss Austria calculate how many days are left with The King.

Top Five Singles

From 1956 through 1962, every new single Elvis released reached the Top Five. This is an incredible twenty-four consecutive Top Five hits! No other artist has ever come close to this record. Asking you to put all twenty-four of these hits in chronological order might be too hard (although for a real challenge, you might try). Instead, we want you to give the year that each song listed below hit the Top Five. It will help you a little to know that there were four Top Five hits in 1956, 1957, 1958, and 1961, three in 1960 and 1962, and two in 1959.

1. "A Big Hunk o' Love" _____
2. "A Fool Such as I" _____
3. "All Shook Up" _____
4. "Are You Lonesome Tonight?" _____
5. "Can't Help Falling in Love" _____
6. "Don't" _____
7. "Don't Be Cruel" _____
8. "Good Luck Charm" _____
9. "Hard Headed Woman" _____
10. "Heartbreak Hotel" _____
11. "I Feel So Bad" _____
12. "I Want You, I Need You, I Love You" _____

13. "It's Now or Never" _____
14. "Jailhouse Rock" _____
15. "Little Sister" _____
16. "Love Me Tender" _____
17. "One Night" _____
18. "Return to Sender" _____
19. "She's Not You" _____
20. "Stuck on You" _____
21. "Surrender" _____
22. "Teddy Bear" _____
23. "Too Much" _____
24. "Wear My Ring Around Your Neck" _____

Bonus Question: Three of these singles were two-sided Top Five hits. Identify those three singles and name the flip side of each.

★ **Elvis and Priscilla spent their honeymoon in Palm Springs, California. And Sonny Bono wasn't even the mayor!**

★ **Elvis's first Las Vegas engagement at the New Frontier in 1956 proved to be unsuccessful and was cut short.**

★ Movie Roles

Elvis portrayed a wide variety of characters during his movie career. Try to match the title of each of these films with the role that Elvis played in that movie. (If you're a fan of Elvis's music, but not his movies, this quiz may be difficult for you.)

_____ 1. *Change of Habit*

_____ 2. *Charro!*

_____ 3. *Clambake*

_____ 4. *Easy Come, Easy Go*

_____ 5. *Flaming Star*

_____ 6. *Frankie and Johnny*

_____ 7. *Fun in Acapulco*

_____ 8. *G.I. Blues*

_____ 9. *Girl Happy*

_____ 10. *Girls! Girls! Girls!*

_____ 11. *It Happened at the World's Fair*

_____ 12. *Kid Galahad*

_____ 13. *Kissin' Cousins*

_____ 14. *Live a Little, Love a Little*

_____ 15. *Paradise, Hawaiian Style*

_____ 16. *Roustabout*

_____ 17. *Tickle Me*

_____ 18. *Viva Las Vegas*

A. air force officer/hillbilly

B. airline pilot

C. army tank gunner

D. boxer

E. charter boat captain

F. crop duster

G. doctor in the slums

H. former gang outlaw

I. half-breed Indian

J. navy frogman

K. night club entertainer

L. photographer

M. race car driver

N. riverboat gambler

O. rodeo rider

P. son of oil millionaire

Q. trapeze artist and lifeguard

R. vagabond carnival singer

Bonus Question: In addition to one of the movies in the list above, name two other movies in which Elvis played a race car driver.

★ **During his four-week series of concerts at the Las Vegas International Hotel in 1969, Elvis outdrew Frank Sinatra, Dean Martin, and Barbra Streisand. Not a single seat was unsold.**

Elvis Covers Songs of Other Artists

During the first dozen years at RCA, Elvis recorded primarily new songs. Later in his career, he began to perform and record ("cover") numerous songs that had already been big hits for someone else. The twenty such songs below were recorded by twenty different artists. Name the artists who originally recorded these songs. (The dates in parentheses refer to the years that the songs first appeared as Elvis recordings.)

1. "And I Love You So" (1975) _____

2. "Are You Sincere" (1973) _____

3. "Fairytale" (1975) _____

4. "Gentle on My Mind" (1969) _____

5. "Hurt" (1976) _____

6. "I Can Help" (1975) _____

7. "I Just Can't Help Believin'" (1970) _____

8. "It Keeps Right on A-Hurtin'" (1969) _____

9. "Love Letters" (1966) _____

10. "Mary in the Morning" (1970) _____

11. "Never Been to Spain" (1972) _____

12. "Only the Strong Survive" (1969) _____

13. "Polk Salad Annie" (1970) _____

14. "Put Your Hand in the Hand" (1972) _____

15. "Runaway" (1970) _____

16. "Sweet Caroline" (1970) _____

17. "Walk a Mile in My Shoes" (1970) _____

18. "The Wonder of You" (1970) _____

19. "Words" (1969) _____

20. "You Don't Have to Say You Love Me" (1970) _____

Bonus Question: Name three number-one hits by the Beatles that were later recorded by Elvis. A fourth number-one hit by the Beatles was sometimes used by Elvis in concert as a tag to one of his own hits. What was that song?

★ 18 A Country Elvis

Elvis was a small-town boy who had deep country roots. Both sides of two Sun singles in 1955 made the country charts before he had his first pop hit, "Heartbreak Hotel." In the 1970s, Elvis recorded many country-flavored songs. See if you can unscramble the titles of the country songs below. To make the quiz easier and more informative, for each scrambled title three pieces of information are provided: the name of the country artist who had a big country hit with the song, the year it was released by that artist, and the year it was released by Elvis. Note that these eighteen songs were recorded by eighteen different *country artists.*

1. I KNTISH HES RAEC LILTS

   _____

   Released by George Jones in 1962, by Elvis in 1977

2. HET ETSMI DOGO ROF

   _____

   Released by Ray Price in 1970, by Elvis in 1972

3. HES HNWE EIRDT NSSAU

   _____

   Released by the Statler Brothers in 1974, by Elvis in 1975

4. YM TO LRDWO OEWLEMC

   _____

   Released by Jim Reeves in 1964, by Elvis in 1974

5. YGCNRI ETH NRIA SEEY NI ULEB

   _____

   Released by Willie Nelson in 1975, by Elvis in 1976

6. A DAHN EHKSA

   _____

   Released by Red Foley in 1953, by Elvis in 1975

7. HTE UATOB STMIE DOOG LAKT

   _____

   Released by Jerry Reed in 1970, by Elvis in 1974

8. DEPRA

   _____

   Released by Marty Robbins in 1971, by Elvis in 1973

9. NO 'MI NOMIV'

   _____

   Released by Hank Snow in 1950, by Elvis in 1969

10. YM SEOG NEGVYREIHT REEHT

Released by Jack Greene in 1966,
by Elvis in 1970

_____

11. WKON 'NDTO EM UYO

Released by Jerry Vale in 1956,
by Elvis in 1967

_____

12. TI HNGTI EM HHTGRUO KAEM ETH PHLE

Released by Sammi Smith in 1970,
by Elvis in 1972

_____

13. THRAE RYUO 'TNCEHAI

Released by Hank Williams in 1953,
by Elvis in 1965

_____

14. FO SAGRS ENERG MOEH NERGE

Released by Porter Wagoner in 1965,
by Elvis in 1975

_____

15. DLRO YHW EM

Released by Kris Kristofferson in 1973,
by Elvis in 1974

_____

16. POTS UYO I 'TANC GLVONI

Released by Don Gibson in 1958,
by Elvis in 1969

_____

17. REEVN ROROMOWT ECMSO

Released by Ernest Tubb in 1945,
by Elvis in 1971

_____

18. A A OT GINK ORMF KJCA

Released by Ned Miller in 1962,
by Elvis in 1969

_____

★ Grenada, the country the United States invaded in 1983, once honored Elvis on a postage stamp.

★ Dolores Hart, who was in _Loving You_ and starred with George Hamilton in the 1961 hit _Where the Boys Are,_ quit acting to become a nun in 1963.

Top Ten Hits

Elvis had thirty-eight Top Ten pop hits—more than any other artist. Eighteen of these songs reached the coveted number-one spot on Billboard's pop charts, but the other twenty didn't. The titles of sixteen of these twenty songs are hidden horizontally, vertically, and diagonally in the square below. No title is displayed backward. This word-search puzzle should be a little more difficult than the earlier word search, Elvis Is Number One.

```
L N T L Z B Y R H E F M G Q C A L Y P Y R Y X I L
V C L R M X T G W W P I K L F O G Z E M T H A T O
P W K V Y W V K L O V E M E L T L G G O I V J O B
C C T Y R X Y V J X E H I S L A T E S T F L A M E
V J R E T U R N T O S E N D E R G F T Y E X Z J O
X E R H E G K C E H D C K E R O B G D F E V H Z E
B F P T H T T H E W O N D E R O F Y O U L B B K L
K Z P W E M T T Z T Q M S L S Q F A Q S R D Z Z
Q T F B A Q H U T Z U S T H F S A S F F O Z A B N
O B R E C G I E E N I Y A E Y L L O O G B N V O O
Y S U E I J H M Q S D B O S V X Y T O I A Y K O F
K U C N V G V B E D E M F N T V P N L L D C R I A
Y E E Z E A K L A V C Y H O R U H B S B C H K O I
F N M H Y U T D I G O T S T U N G O U U H Z G J U
O R T J G T Y K U F U A E Y K S C S C R A D F Q S
W N W C I R G E P A T S Y O H S Y S H N R I U G B
I I Z L C I V V W M B K H U F Y L A A I L M Q P P
B G E T L T R I N H L V P A P F W N S N O R G N A
B L N M X W S N H L A G M J U K P O I G T G F S T
R O B G B H F D D A A I H T H V F V T L T T D A A
D Q D E V I L I N D I S G U I S E A C O E R S Q G
N L X J H P Z Y C G U A M H T S T B S V Z E X D C
P C U P W Z J V Z G C R T P S B V A W E S C V G F
L K W D K H U L L Q T E D X B T A B Y X S K N K U
Y E E T D I B E G O F Y O U S E B Y D Y E Q A S T
```

Ten British Singles

Elvis was not only a rock & roll sensation in the United States, he was also extremely popular in England. Ten song titles are scrambled below. Most of these songs were never released as singles in the United States, but all of them reached the Top Twenty as singles in Great Britain. Prove your worldliness by unscrambling the titles.

1. REEVY FI KILE TSMCHASRI SAW YDA

_____

2. EEOLCR NIKG

_____

3. OT TLO 'O TOG VLIIN' A OD

_____

4. DWLAY WADLCY SIMS

_____

5. FO RIGL TESB YM EIRDNF

_____

6. TAREH DONEOW

_____

7. LEPH 'TANC I 'IVBELNIE TJSU

_____

8. GRINB KBCA TANAS MY BYBA

_____

9. OT RINTY' OT OYU TEG

_____

10. TARPY

_____

Bonus Question: One of these songs was released as a B side in the United States but did not make the Top One Hundred. However, it was awarded a Gold record for sales of more than one million copies in Europe. Which song was it?

Lots of Plots

Undoubtedly, most of you have seen many of Elvis's efforts from Tinseltown. Some loyalists have probably even seen several of the King's films more than once. Although critics frequently panned his movies, Elvis did some fine work at times, especially in such films as King Creole *and* Flaming Star. *Try to match each of the following plot descriptions with the appropriate movie title.*

_____ 1. While in the army, Elvis bets his friends that he can spend the night with Lili, a cabaret dancer. She is angry when she learns about the bet, but all ends well as Elvis and Lili fall in love.

_____ 2. Elvis plays the operator of a helicopter taxi service who gets in trouble with the Federal Aviation Administration but redeems himself after he performs a rescue mission.

_____ 3. A pretty psychiatrist/social worker helps Elvis control his hotheadedness and develop his literary talent.

_____ 4. A very wealthy Elvis trades identities with a poor man in an effort to learn whether people like him for himself or for his money.

_____ 5. Elvis is hired to chaperone the sexy daughter of a Fort Lauderdale underworld character named Big Frank.

_____ 6. Loosely based on Elvis's own life, this movie depicts a small-town boy whose upbeat music gets him top billing with a touring band.

_____ 7. Elvis is a race car driver who, while being investigated by the Internal Revenue Service, woos a female IRS agent.

_____ 8. As the leader of a group of traveling entertainers in the Roaring Twenties, Elvis must deal with murder, kidnapping, and union problems.

_____ 9. Elvis learns to play the guitar in prison, but later he becomes a greedy and cantankerous star. A blow to the throat nearly ends his career and brings him to his senses.

_____ 10. Elvis plays a young nightclub singer who gets sucked into the New Orleans underworld.

_____ 11. Elvis is a lifeguard and entertainer caught between two women—one a bullfighter, the other a hotel social director. In one memorable scene, he conquers his fear of heights by diving off a tall cliff.

_____ 12. Elvis and his eccentric, poor family decide to homestead in southern Florida.

_____ 13. Although heir to his parents' pineapple empire, Elvis goes to work in the tourism business to prove he can support himself.

_____ 14. This period piece, set in the late 1800s, features Elvis as a half-breed in the middle of a race war between whites and Indians.

_____ 15. Elvis is out of work while at an all-female dude ranch. He escapes the advances of most of the women and finds hidden gold.

_____ 16. In this Civil War movie, Elvis plays one of four Confederate brothers with different political beliefs but the same love interest.

A. *Blue Hawaii*

B. *Clambake*

C. *Flaming Star*

D. *Follow That Dream*

E. *Fun in Acapulco*

F. *G.I. Blues*

G. *Girl Happy*

H. *Jailhouse Rock*

I. *King Creole*

J. *Love Me Tender*

K. *Loving You*

L. *Paradise, Hawaiian Style*

M. *Speedway*

N. *Tickle Me*

O. *The Trouble with Girls*

P. *Wild in the Country*

After his films had sold more popcorn than any other movies in 1956 and 1957, the star is given a Kernel's commission on the mayor's staff of Nashville's Popcorn Village.

The King of Rock & Roll sports trimmed sideburns in 1958 to prepare for his fourth movie, *King Creole*.

★ The 1973 satellite presentation of "Elvis: Aloha from Hawaii" had an estimated worldwide viewing audience of more than one billion people.

Important Elvis Dates

In this quiz, when we talk about dates, we're not talking about females but rather about important times in Elvis's life. It's up to you to come up with the appropriate dates for the events mentioned. Unless otherwise instructed, you are only required to list the year. Points will be awarded and you can evaluate your performance. Unless otherwise stated, a question is worth one point.

_____ 1. Date Elvis was born (month, day, and year)

_____ 2. Date of Elvis's death (month, day, and year)

_____ 3. Year he married Priscilla (one bonus point for month)

_____ 4. Birth of Lisa Marie (one bonus point for month)

_____ 5. Year he was divorced from Priscilla

_____ 6. Death of Elvis's mother (one bonus point for month)

_____ 7. Induction into army (one bonus point for month)

_____ 8. First commercial recording session (one bonus point for month)

_____ 9. Elvis gives a benefit concert that will be his last live performance until 1968 (one bonus point for month)

_____ 10. First gold record released (one bonus point for month)

_____ 11. Unsuccessful audition for "Arthur Godfrey's Talent Scouts" (one bonus point for month)

_____ 12. First appearance on "The Ed Sullivan Show" (one bonus point for month)

_____ 13. Elvis's New York press conference held before his Madison Square Garden concerts (two points)

_____ 14. Premiere of his first movie (one bonus point for month)

_____ 15. First concert in Las Vegas (one bonus point for month)

_____ 16. Last single in the pop Top Forty

★ **Lisa Marie was born exactly nine months after Elvis's marriage to Priscilla.**

★ 23 David's Favorites

While individuals tend to associate a singer with a particular period of their lives, Elvis produced hits over so many years that many of us grew into adulthood still listening to new releases. Amazing! Anyhow, here I go with my favorites. Most are bigger hits and better-known songs than those on Kent's list, which appears later in this book. See if you can unscramble the titles from the descriptions that are provided.

1. The title of this bouncy song with very clever lyrics became a slang phrase used throughout the country. The background music includes an interesting slapping noise that appears on several Elvis records. The song is about a guy who is so in love that he feels great, but also a little strange.

   KOSOH PU LAL

   _____

2. This is a country-rock story-song from the 1970s about a man trying to trace the whereabouts of his girlfriend. Listen for the thunder in the background.

   NARI TCUKNEYK

   _____

3. This song is also country flavored and has a sweet but somewhat sad sound. It tells the story of a man who really cares about a woman, but doesn't want to tell her. It was the B side of a 1962 single.

   REH ISDA MJI LELT LEHOL SUTJ

   _____

4. Another popular song from the early 1960s with catchy words and a gentle beat. Elvis sings about some problems getting mail delivered.

   DSREEN TRNERU OT

   _____

5. This song is melodic, sweet, and sad. Elvis sounds lonesome as he sings sensitively about a man who is an unhappy wanderer. It was the B side of a 1961 number-one hit.

   NMA YEONLL

   _____

6. When Elvis performed ferocious rock songs like this one, it is no wonder adults were perplexed. This song is light-years from the standard bland fare that was being recorded by many artists just a few years before. Today, it is vintage rock & roll with a compelling beat and amusing lyrics. When performed in one of Elvis's early movies, it was the basis of probably the best dance routine he ever did.

   CKOR SHJLOAUIE

   _____

7. I really like the lyrics and the great beat of this song from the early 1960s. (I give it a 96.) It tells of a man who thinks his lover is true and then sadly discovers she is seeing someone else. Although her new boyfriend brags, he most certainly faces heartbreak ahead.

EMFAL TTALSE SIH

_____

8. This song never became a blockbuster hit by Elvis's standards, but it is my favorite of the King's ballads. He sang it on one of his television specials before it was released as a single. Romantic and reminiscent, the lyrics remind me of those in *The Way We Were* by Barbra Streisand.

SMOMREIE

_____

9. This giant hit is simply a wonderful song that Elvis performed masterfully, his vocal style bordering on operatic. It is typical of the shift in Elvis's music from rock to ballads after his return from the army. For those few who still don't believe that Elvis could really sing, this song should convince them otherwise. The words are sung gently, but the song builds to a big, majestic conclusion.

RO WNO VRNEE STI'

_____

10. This nice soft rock & roll song was a huge hit for Elvis early in his career, and still is one of the tunes for which he is most remembered. The song has a steady beat and features vocal tricks by the King and great background work by the Jordanaires.

UCLRE 'TOND EB

_____

★ For several years, Elvis wouldn't watch the movie *Loving You*. His beloved mother had a bit part in the film, and it hurt him too much to be reminded that she was no longer alive.

★ The song "Danny," which was originally intended to be the title song for *King Creole,* was recorded by Elvis in 1958 but not released until 1978. Meanwhile, Conway Twitty had a Top 10 hit with the song in 1960 under the title "Lonely Blue Boy."

Songs from Movies

The A and/or B sides of many of Elvis's singles came from his movies. Several, such as "Love Me Tender," "Jailhouse Rock," and "Kissin' Cousins" are movie title songs. If you want to find out how much you know about Elvis's movies, match each of the following songs with the movie in which Elvis sang it.

_____	1. "Teddy Bear"	A.	*Blue Hawaii*
_____	2. "Let Yourself Go"	B.	*Change of Habit*
_____	3. "You Don't Know Me"	C.	*Clambake*
_____	4. "Do the Clam"	D.	*Double Trouble*
_____	5. "Bossa Nova Baby"	E.	*Frankie and Johnny*
_____	6. "What'd I Say"	F.	*Fun in Acapulco*
_____	7. "All That I Am"	G.	*G.I. Blues*
_____	8. "Hard Headed Woman"	H.	*Girl Happy*
_____	9. "Easy Question"	I.	*Girls! Girls! Girls!*
_____	10. "Rubberneckin'"	J.	*It Happened at the World's Fair*
_____	11. "Clean Up Your Own Back Yard"	K.	*Jailhouse Rock*
_____	12. "Wooden Heart"	L.	*King Creole*
_____	13. "Return to Sender"	M.	*Live a Little, Love a Little*
_____	14. "Please Don't Stop Loving Me"	N.	*Loving You*
_____	15. "Treat Me Nice"	O.	*Speedway*
_____	16. "Can't Help Falling in Love"	P.	*Spinout*
_____	17. "Long Legged Girl"	Q.	*Tickle Me*
_____	18. "One Broken Heart for Sale"	R.	*The Trouble with Girls*
_____	19. "A Little Less Conversation"	S.	*Viva Las Vegas*

★ **Country music star Jerry Reed wrote two Elvis hits, "U.S. Male" and "Guitar Man." He also played lead guitar for these recordings.**

Early Acquaintances of the King

As a young man, Elvis came into contact with a number of interesting individuals, many of whom played an important part in the entertainer's later life. See how many of Elvis's friends you can identify in the following word search. Each of the twenty individuals whose names are hidden in the puzzle played a part in Elvis's life before he was drafted by the U.S. Army. To make this puzzle a little easier, no names are displayed diagonally.

```
B D H W M Z Q C A H G T Y D F L M E A G G C R Z R
T J M E I T K V S P G C Q L N V J K J M B B D P Q K
F V Y O B X S N C M F D D U D J F O N T A N A Z N
R E D W E S T C O W D L L J G L T A N K N U T D M
B S E I J A C C T Z E E G L D I D B P R J I E G H
R I U T X M D C T E S X L P K M C J J D S R U L F
U I E W F P O J Y S W T J Q S K O A A J D N Y A Y
P H A V D H V S M F I Z N H I L R L V J T C J D D
M D T V R I M Z O N N J U Y K S S J M B Z L R Y C
A M Q N N L X A O C K J E R R Y L E E L E W I S W
E M X R N L V C R U M P R D U Q Y M Y L U S P S Q
A U V R U I Y R E N A K J L E M R F B Z R M O M C
X B E O B P R K U N R S T E V E A L L E N Y D I A
T I S Y P S B V S O T P G O T I P L M P V K O T R
O L T O A S O F C G I J Z C Z S C K H E G Z Z H L
N L E R T E B E T D N V J I T C K X A E V G R X P
O B R B B I N M Z U D T O M M Y D O R S E Y T Q E
O L P I O O E Z P U A D E W E Y P H I L L I P S R
B A R S O W A X Z P L J A E D S U L L I V A N Q K
C C E O N U L M D X E F F T K O C L F Q E P F Y I
T K S N E I M U P V R X C Q R I O O H P J E M F N
Y B L U A G B M G B J P I P L G B B Z M J E B B S
U P E J O H N N Y C A S H T O M P A R K E R D R B
Y X Y N I Y N S Z P M J Q R A K F A S N J T Q V W
B X K Y U O Y T J F R S G U E V C M L Y N C N S Y
```

★ Descriptive Song Titles

Some of Elvis's song titles are so descriptive that it is fun to play around with the words and see if you can come up with something a little different that says the same thing. Kay Scott played around with some Elvis tunes and came up with the following. See if you're on her wavelength. In a few of the more difficult questions, supplemental clues are given.

1. ←———————— WAYS   WAYS ————————→

   _____

2. Gentle
   My Mind

   _____

3. 2 x Trouble

   _____

4. ?   Train

   _____

5. BOSS MAN

   _____

6. Blame ————————→ _____
                          Me

   (On the 1961 *Something for Everybody* album)

   _____

7. sister

   _____

8. LOVE LOVE LOVE LOVE LOVE
   (A bonus song on the *Kissin' Cousins* album)

   _____

9. L I (first) N E

   (On Elvis's second album)

   _____

40

10. Sleepy   Sleepy   Sleepy   Sleepy   Sleepy
    Head   Head   Head   Head   Head

_____

11. M O U N   (gold)   T A I N S

(On the *Kissin' Cousins* album)

_____

12. RAGS   ⟶   Riches

_____

13. # SALLY

_____

14. American   American   American

_____

15. <u>1, 2, 3, 4, 5, . . .</u>
          You

(On Elvis's first album)

_____

★   Lisa Marie's middle name was chosen to honor Colonel Tom Parker's wife.

★   *Billboard* named "It's Now or Never" the vocal single of the year for 1960.

⭐ 27 Songwriting Teams

Jerry Leiber and Mike Stoller were a very productive songwriting team. Some of their songs listed below were first recorded by other artists, but most of them were written specifically for Elvis. Mort Shuman and Doc Pomus, another prolific songwriting team, penned songs for the likes of Dion and the Belmonts, Fabian, the Drifters, Gary "U.S." Bonds, Terry Stafford, and, of course, the King. The first thirteen Elvis songs below were written by Leiber and Stoller and the last seven were written by Shuman and Pomus. Match each song with the correct description.

_____ 1. "Hound Dog"

_____ 2. "Love Me"

_____ 3. "Loving You"

_____ 4. "Dirty, Dirty Feeling"

_____ 5. "Bossa Nova Baby"

_____ 6. "Steadfast, Loyal and True"

_____ 7. "Just Tell Her Jim Said Hello"

_____ 8. "Fools Fall in Love"

_____ 9. "Jailhouse Rock"

_____ 10. "Don't"

_____ 11. "Little Egypt"

_____ 12. "Saved"

_____ 13. "King Creole"

_____ 14. "What Every Woman Lives For"

_____ 15. "Doin' the Best I Can"

_____ 16. "Double Trouble"

_____ 17. "His Latest Flame"

_____ 18. "Little Sister"

_____ 19. "Surrender"

_____ 20. "Viva Las Vegas"

A. From *G.I. Blues*

B. Ode to a high school

C. His heart was on fire, and hers was too.

D. About a woman with long, black hair

E. Title of a 1967 movie

F. In this song, unlike "Don't Be Cruel," Elvis was willing to be treated cruelly.

G. When she was younger, she had pigtails and a turned-up nose.

H. Title of Elvis's second movie

I. Top Forty hit for the Coasters

J. Flip side of "Indescribably Blue"

K. From *Tickle Me*

L. Title of Elvis's third movie

M. Didn't have high class

N. Title of Elvis's fourth movie

O. A Top Ten hit in 1963

P. Recorded by LaVern Baker

Q. A hit single and the title of a 1964 movie

R. Flip side of "She's Not You"

S. Sung in *Frankie and Johnny*

T. A number-one hit in 1958

Private Presley receives a hug from a German teenager in 1958.

Elvis stands beside the used BMW he purchased in 1958 for $3,750.

★ **Caroline Kennedy covered Elvis's funeral as a photojournalist for** *Rolling Stone.*

Top Forty Gems

Elvis had more than fifty songs that made the Top Forty but not the Top Ten. Unscramble the titles of the Top Forty songs listed below.

1. NEKROB LAES ROF NEO TREAH

   _____

2. SOSB IGB NAM

   _____

3. ESNIOTQU YEAS

   _____

4. OYU STOL VEI'

   _____

5. KAS YHW TOND' EM

   _____

6. SEEPK ROF YLPGNIA

   _____

7. DAN TUNEROF MEAF

   _____

8. NIAR TENKKCUY

   _____

9. SRODEIPM DANL

   _____

10. MEAC YM SIHW URET

    _____

11. MALC OD HTE

    _____

12. YYAWAN EM TANW OUY

    _____

13. EM YM TELF YABB

    _____

14. LETL HWY EM

    _____

15. EERHW OG DORL IDD HETY

    _____

16. EM SIKS CIUKQ

    _____

17. PU DARY NOW NEALC UROY KABC

    _____

18. LRTEAMSLREO EUSBL

    _____

19. 'VEI A UYO BBYA TOG GHINT TAOUB

    _____

20. EM TI SURTH

    _____

★ **TV's "The Gong Show" once dedicated the entire show to Elvis impersonators. If you find it for rent at your local video store, be sure to drop us a line.**

45

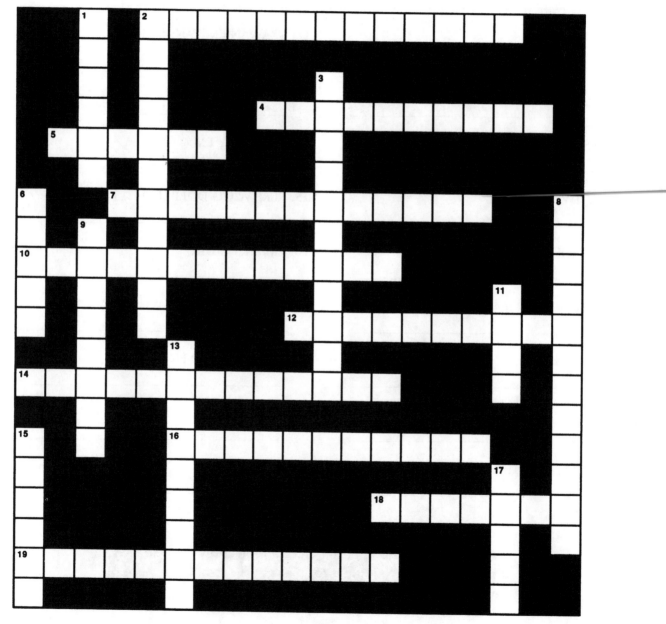

★ Contemporaries of the 1950s

Although there was only one King of Rock & Roll, a lot of other great singers were belting out fine rock & roll during the late 1950s. (Hey, what would it mean to be the King if there weren't any pretenders to the throne?) Test your knowledge of Elvis's early contemporaries by completing this crossword puzzle.

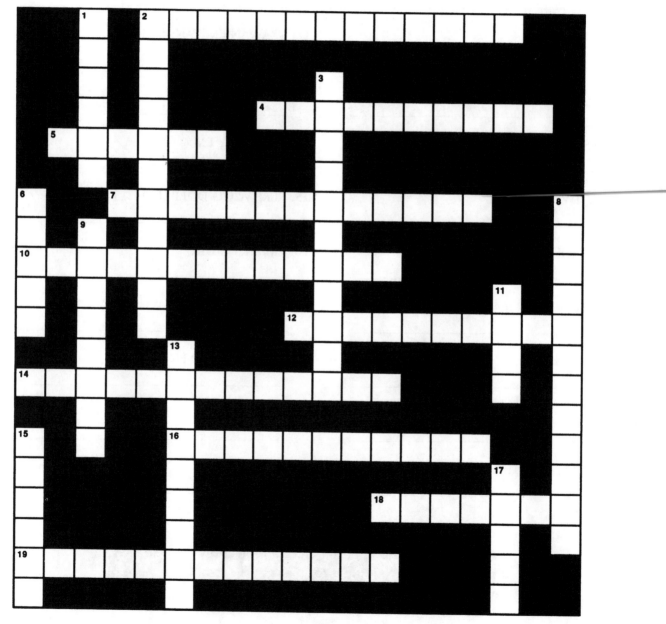

ACROSS

2. She found lipstick on his collar.
4. A giant of early rock & roll even though his first number-one hit didn't occur until 1972
5. "Mr. Excitement," once a singer with the Dominoes (first name)
7. Richard Penniman
10. Andy Williams had a hit with "Butterfly"; this fellow's version was equally big.
12. Had first big hit with "The Diary"
14. He probably would have liked to live on Venus . . . or is it *with* Venus?
16. For him, it was just a matter of time.
18. He decided to go to Kansas City (first name).
19. Leader of the Imperials

DOWN

1. A tiger who requested to be turned loose
2. Had a big hit with "C. C. Rider"
3. Sang the blues till he had heartaches by the number
6. A poor little fool who spent some time in lonesome town (first name)
8. Harold Jenkins, who sounded like Elvis on some early hits
9. She discovered her parents doing the rock & roll waltz.
11. His heart was an open book (first name).
13. J. P. Richardson
15. Proclaimed "We Got Love" (last name)
17. Was left breathless (last name)

The sergeant squires 19-year-old Nancy Sinatra in 1960.

★ In 1985 "Hound Dog" was honored as a "standard" by the American Society of Composers, Authors and Publishers (ASCAP). It joined more subdued songs such as "As Time Goes By" and "Night and Day."

Elvis arrives at Fort Dix, New Jersey, in March 1960 to be discharged from the army.

★ During the summer of 1988, the Nixon Presidential Materials Project received 12,000 requests for a copy of a letter that Elvis sent to Mr. Nixon while he was president.

Elvis, You're More than a Hound Dog

Some of Elvis's songs had the name of an animal in the title, the most famous being "Hound Dog" and "Teddy Bear." In addition, several of his songs mention animals within the lyrics. Match the animals with the songs in which they are mentioned. This quiz will give you yet another excuse to listen to some of your Elvis records.

_____ 1. ants	A. "All Shook Up"
_____ 2. bear, chicken, and possum	B. "Blue Suede Shoes"
_____ 3. bee, kangaroo, mockingbird, and bear	C. "Cindy, Cindy"
_____ 4. black cat	D. "Didja' Ever"
_____ 5. bluebird, bee, and cows	E. "A Dog's Life"
_____ 6. bug	F. "G.I. Blues"
_____ 7. cat	G. "Hound Dog"
_____ 8. chicks, cows, and pigs	H. "How the Web Was Woven"
_____ 9. gators	I. "How Would You Like to Be"
_____ 10. grizzly bear and tiger	J. "I Got Stung"
_____ 11. honeybee	K. "If That Isn't Love"
_____ 12. lamb, lion, wolves, and bear	L. "Mean Woman Blues"
_____ 13. lion and tiger	M. "Old MacDonald"
_____ 14. one-eyed cat	N. "Old Shep"
_____ 15. poodle	O. "Party"
_____ 16. pup and dog	P. "Peace in the Valley"
_____ 17. rabbit	Q. "Polk Salad Annie"
_____ 18. sparrow	R. "Shake, Rattle and Roll"
_____ 19. spider and blue fly	S. "Stuck on You"
_____ 20. Texas cow	T. "Teddy Bear"

★ Stories from Elvis

Some of Elvis's songs, in addition to being enjoyable musically, tell interesting stories. A few are humorous or frivolous, but others are serious, heartbreaking, or profound. Try to match the story lines below with the song titles that follow. Then select the appropriate singles or albums from your collection of Elvis records, pop some popcorn, and have an enjoyable evening snacking and listening to the story songs. Compare the actual lyrics to our descriptions.

_____ 1. I have certainly had a difficult life. My mother died when I was born, and my father blamed me for her being gone. Later I was put in jail even though I was innocent. But the greatest pain was when my wife left me and took my son with her. That was an obstacle that I may never be able to overcome.

_____ 2. It's difficult for me to get out of bed each morning after crying during the night. Sometimes I want to give up, but my children encourage me to laugh and keep going. They like riding on my back and say that we can find a new mommy. But the children hurt too, probably even more than I do, and that doesn't seem fair. I try not to cry and I wonder when the tears will ever end.

_____ 3. Since I was born in Mississippi, I qualify as an American man. I'm angry because you've been chasing my woman. I bought her a ring on sale, and she's mine. If you touch her, I'm going to beat you up. Take my advice: find another woman and don't bother the one that belongs to me.

_____ 4. While it is snowing outside, another baby is being born on the poor side of the city. He needs help as a child to keep him out of trouble later in life. But most of us walk away, refusing to get involved. Sure enough, he gets a gun, steals, and is ultimately killed. Meanwhile, another poverty-stricken baby is born and the cycle begins again.

_____ 5. Our relationship is changing, and we might as well accept the fact that we're no longer meant to be together. We're still friends, but romantic love is gone. Memories of once caring about each other are all that remain now. We'll just part company and perhaps find someone new to love someday. Our daughter will cry when I leave, but maybe she'll understand better when she's older.

_____ 6. The two of us are great lovers, and we promised to never mistreat each other. But I got involved with another woman because I thought she might improve my luck at poker. When my lover found out, she was very angry. She found me in a bar, and even though I begged her not to do it, she shot me. My wound hurts me deeply. I admit my foolish mistake.

_____ 7. I had a great time as a boy playing with my dog. Once he kept me from drowning in the swimming hole. The years flew by and my dog grew old, sick, and nearly blind. The veterinarian advised that he would have to be put to sleep. I cried and wished I could die instead. However, if there's a heaven for dogs, I know that he has a good home now.

_____ 8. Several nights ago, I woke and you were gone. I'm determined to find out why you left, and I want to bring you back. So I'm traveling on lonely roads in bad weather looking for

50

you. Along the way, some old men said they had seen you, but they couldn't remember exactly when. Later, a preacher gave me a ride and prayed that you would be found.

_____ 9. At the time I was born, my dad was in a Georgia jail. As I grew up, he warned me not to end up like he did. I tried to follow his advice, but I started running around with a bad crowd. After I committed a robbery, they locked me up. Impatiently, I broke out of jail, but bloodhounds are after me and I'll probably be back in soon.

_____ 10. When you left our hometown, you said you'd be back someday in a big, fancy car. Well, that dream came true, but certainly not the way that you planned. The newspaper told about your party and fatal car crash. Your rich city friends are mourning as you ride by in a chauffeured car. My eyes are wet with tears, and my dreams of love have died with you.

_____ 11. I told my mother good-bye and quit my hometown job. I hitchhiked all around the Southeast looking for a place to make money using my musical abilities. For quite a while, no one was interested in me. Finally, I got a chance to play in a jam session, and now I'm the leader of a great band in a club in Mobile.

_____ 12. I realize that you're asleep, but this is important and I need to talk to you now. The love that your mom and I had for each other is dead, and I've had all that I can stand. However, I'm willing to stay with you because you're the most important part of my life. You haven't heard anything I said, but maybe it's best that I didn't interrupt your dreams.

_____ 13. When I was a child, neighbors were friendly. We used to spend time with friends at prayer meetings and all-day sing-alongs. Now times are different and most people don't even know their neighbors. My late grandfather was concerned with all the hate in the world and couldn't wait to go to the next life. Someday all these friends from days gone by will sit by the Jordan River and talk together again.

_____ 14. Operator, I need help to get in touch with someone who called me earlier. I don't know her phone number, but her name is Marie and my uncle wrote down her message. I miss her very much after her mother broke up our happy home. When I saw six-year-old Marie last, she was crying; so please find her number quickly.

_____ 15. I make a living playing the piano, and I notice every woman on the dance floor. My mother taught me good manners and did a good job raising nine children by herself. But she never told me how to deal with someone as beautiful as you. I'm sure a lot of men would like to have you, and I bet a lot of women are jealous of you. Fortunately for me, you are still alone.

A. "Don't Cry, Daddy"
B. "Frankie and Johnny"
C. "Guitar Man"
D. "I Washed My Hands in Muddy Water"
E. "In the Ghetto"
F. "Kentucky Rain"
G. "Long Black Limousine"
H. "Memphis, Tennessee"
I. "My Boy"
J. "Old Shep"
K. "Separate Ways"
L. "Talk About the Good Times"
M. "T-R-O-U-B-L-E"
N. "U.S. Male"
O. "You Gave Me a Mountain"

Titles of Gospel Songs

Elvis began singing in the First Assembly of God Church in Tupelo at a very early age. In fact, at the age of two, he would run down the aisle, stand by the choir, and try to sing with them. He paid tribute to his religious roots by recording more than fifty gospel hymns and spirituals. The titles of twenty-two Elvis gospel recordings are hidden horizontally, vertically, and diagonally in this puzzle. See how many you can find.

```
W R U O A D G K C B M N P A T S Y I S G R E A T
E S T S I N T H E G A R D E N I P H S F H L K O
M B W C O E K A Y I S N I C E D N O L P H A N R
A W H I S H A N D I N M I N E O T W H E B J O D
N E Y I N O I G R I T S F U N A R G T A M O W N
S P M A R G T G M A R Y T U A R N R I C B S N Y
I H E R A Y D Q H A Z P R U C T L E J E G H O N
O Y L N H E T O U C H E D M E B V A J I T U N P
N O O C G E K L W F W A J D V B M T O N P A L G
O N R K C I T I S N O S E C R E T T O T A F Y E
V L D C A F B R A J S Y O P N D E H Q H A I T A
E Y O U L L N E V E R W A L K A L O N E I T O M
R B A W G K N B L T Y A E O L P C U F V Y T H A
T E F H N A R E B I N A T E B A C A D A T H I Z
H L A Q W G M F D Y E I R N T E C R V L T E M I
E I E B I P A K B L O V B A F C A T H L Y B R N
H E B Y L O C D A E H L E D B N H Y G E C A Y G
I V X E A B N W I T H O U T H I M A C Y D T E G
L E H F H A G I L N P R T V U W B A R E C T O R
L A C R Y I N G I N T H E C H A P E L I D L E A
T I O B D A V I D I S T H R I F T Y N R O E T C
O P U T Y O U R H A N D I N T H E H A N D T R E
P D O N T Y O U L I K E T H I S W O R D F I N D
```

52

Songs from Times Past

Several of the songs that Elvis recorded were based on songs that had been written many years earlier. See if you are able to name the appropriate songs from the descriptions that are provided below.

1. Based on "Aura Lee," a traditional song written during the Civil War, this was an early Elvis hit.

   _____

2. Based on "O Sole Mio," an Italian song written in 1901, this was a 1960 multimillion seller for the King.

   _____

3. Based on another Italian ballad called "Come Back to Sorrento," this was written in 1911 and proved to be yet another major hit for Elvis, in 1961.

   _____

4. An Irish song written in 1913 and adapted from "Londonderry Air," this song has been recorded by many artists over the years. Elvis recorded it for a 1976 album.

   _____

5. This is a Christmas carol written in France in the late 1700s under the title "Adeste Fideles."

   _____

6. Based on a nineteenth-century ballad that was first printed in 1904 under the title "He Done Me Wrong," this became the title song for an Elvis movie.

   _____

7. Based on the classical "Plaisir d'Amour" and written more than 150 years ago, this song was a hit single for Elvis, who sang it in *Blue Hawaii.*

   _____

★ **Elvis's middle name, Aaron, was inadvertently spelled with a single *A* on his birth certificate. This incorrect spelling, *Aron*, was later used on an album release, even though throughout his life Elvis spelled it *Aaron*.**

⭐ Name That Album

34

During his busy career, Elvis recorded more than six hundred songs on more than seventy-five albums. Few recording artists can even approach these astonishing numbers. Elvis's productivity has surely resulted in a whole lot of listening pleasure, but it makes this quiz more difficult. See if you can name the album that contains each group of songs listed below.

1. "Hurt"
   "Solitaire"
   "Blue Eyes Crying in the Rain"
   _____

2. "In the Ghetto"
   "It Keeps Right on A-Hurtin'"
   "Long Black Limousine"
   _____

3. "I Got a Woman"
   "Tutti Frutti"
   "Money Honey"
   _____

4. "Judy"
   "It's a Sin"
   "Sentimental Me"
   _____

5. "Playing for Keeps"
   "My Baby Left Me"
   "I Was the One"
   _____

6. "Your Cheatin' Heart"
   "Memphis, Tennessee"
   "Santa Lucia"
   _____

7. "Way Down"
   "Unchained Melody"
   "He'll Have to Go"
   _____

8. "Bringing It Back"
   "I Can Help"
   "And I Love You So"
   _____

9. "Love Me"
   "Rip It Up"
   "Old Shep"
   _____

10. "The Girl of My Best Friend"
    "Such a Night"
    "Soldier Boy"   _____

11. "Young and Beautiful"
    "Is It So Strange"
    "We're Gonna Move"   _____

12. "Help Me"
    "There's a Honky Tonk Angel"
    "You Asked Me To"   _____

13. "Help Me Make It Through the Night"
    "Fools Rush In"
    "Until It's Time for You to Go"   _____

14. "Snowbird"
    "Whole Lotta Shakin' Goin' On"
    "There Goes My Everything"   _____

15. "Kiss Me Quick"
    "(Such an) Easy Question"
    "Suspicion"   _____

16. "Release Me"
    "Runaway"
    "The Wonder of You"   _____

17. "Heart of Rome"
    "Life"
    "Got My Mojo Working"   _____

18. "Are You Sincere"
    "For Ol' Times Sake"
    "I Miss You"   _____

19. "Spanish Eyes"
    "My Boy"
    "Take Good Care of Her"   _____

20. "I Just Can't Help Believin'"
    "I've Lost You"
    "Mary in the Morning"   _____

Word Pictures

Kay Scott, David's wife, who was a cheerleader and a Miss CHS while at Clearwater (Florida) High School, has struck again. She has taken the Descriptive Song Titles quiz a step further by creating drawings that describe titles of Elvis hits. Beside each word picture below, write the name of the song that was on her mind. For harder questions or more obscure songs, an additional clue is provided.

1. ASK ME WHY

_____

2.

_____
Sung in *Follow That Dream*

3.

_____

4. Creole

_____

5.

_____

6.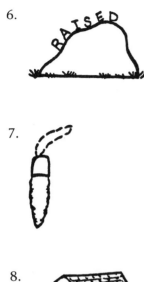

The A side of a 1973 single and title of a 1973 album

7.

Number 1 hit in 1962

8.

9.

1964 hit for Tommy Tucker

10.

Classic Bob Wills country song

11.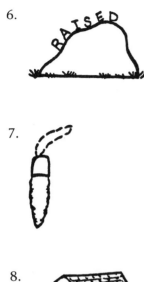

Peter, Paul, and Mary tune sung in the *Aloha from Hawaii* TV special

12.

Gale Storm hit not released by Elvis during his lifetime

_____

13.

B side of a 1970 single

_____

14.

_____

15.

_____

Quotes About Elvis

Not many individuals—not even those involved in the entertainment industry—have generated more public attention and comment than Elvis. Below are a number of interesting quotations concerning the King of Rock & Roll. See if you can match each quotation with the individual who reportedly made the statement.

_____ 1. "Nothing really affected me until Elvis."

_____ 2. "His music and his personality, fusing the styles of the white country and black rhythm & blues, permanently changed the face of American popular culture."

_____ 3. "The kid has no right behaving like a sex maniac on a national show."

_____ 4. "He had created his own world. He had to. There was nothing else for him to do."

_____ 5. "He taught white America to get down."

_____ 6. "If I could find a white man who had the Negro sound and the Negro feel, I could make a million dollars."

_____ 7. "You Memphis politicians had better watch out if Elvis Presley ever decides to enter politics."

_____ 8. "Mr. Presley has no discernible singing ability."

_____ 9. "I wouldn't have Presley on my show at any time."

_____ 10. "From what I've heard, I'm not so sure I'd want my children to see him."

_____ 11. "The voice covers about two octaves and a third, from the baritone's low G to the tenor's high B . . . In ballads and country songs, he belts out full-voiced high G's and A's that an opera baritone might enjoy."

_____ 12. "Without Elvis, none of us could have made it."

_____ 13. "My gosh, you're guarded better than the president!"

_____ 14. "Elvis is the greatest blues singer in the world today."

_____ 15. "To measure a man by his smallest deed or weakest link is like measuring the power of the ocean by a single wave."

A. Kathy Westmoreland
B. Jack Gould (*New York Times*)
C. Ed Sullivan
D. Joe Cocker
E. James Brown
F. Sam Phillips
G. Buddy Holly
H. Johnny Rivers

I. John Lennon
J. Billy Graham
K. Henry Pleasants (vocal critic)
L. George Bush
M. Jackie Gleason
N. Billy Carter
O. Jimmy Carter

On the Country Charts

Most of the Elvis tunes listed below would not normally be considered country songs, but they made the country charts nevertheless. What makes these songs even more unusual is that they never made the pop charts! Match the titles with the descriptions.

_____ 1. "Always on My Mind"	A. It stole his girlfriend.
_____ 2. "Are You Sincere"	B. From *Loving You*
_____ 3. "Baby, Let's Play House"	C. Flip side of "Burning Love"
_____ 4. "Help Me"	D. Andy Williams hit
_____ 5. "I Forgot to Remember to Forget"	E. Flip side of "Way Down"
_____ 6. "I Got a Feelin' in My Body"	F. Hit for the Righteous Brothers
_____ 7. "I'm Left, You're Right, She's Gone"	G. Flip side of "Promised Land"
_____ 8. "It's a Matter of Time"	H. A religious request
_____ 9. "It's Midnight"	I. Hit for Willie Nelson
_____ 10. "Loving Arms"	J. Sad, introspective song
_____ 11. "Mean Woman Blues"	K. Flip side of Elvis's first charted record
_____ 12. "Mystery Train"	L. Hit for the Carpenters
_____ 13. "Pieces of My Life"	M. Hit for Waylon Jennings
_____ 14. "Pledging My Love"	N. Number-one Elvis hit in 1955
_____ 15. "Softly, as I Leave You"	O. Hit for Conway Twitty
_____ 16. "Solitaire"	P. Playful 1955 Elvis hit
_____ 17. "There's a Honky Tonk Angel"	Q. Upbeat spiritual
_____ 18. "Unchained Melody"	R. Country hit in 1963 for Carl Butler and Pearl
_____ 19. "You Asked Me To"	S. Sherrill Nielsen sings and Elvis talks.

★ **Blind country singer Ronnie Milsap sang a duet with Elvis on "Don't Cry, Daddy."**

To the Movies Again

Now that you have had experience locating movie titles in an earlier quiz, you may be able to find these titles a little more quickly. There are twelve titles in the puzzle below. (Don't forget to look for the two Elvis documentaries that followed his acting finale in film number twenty-nine.)

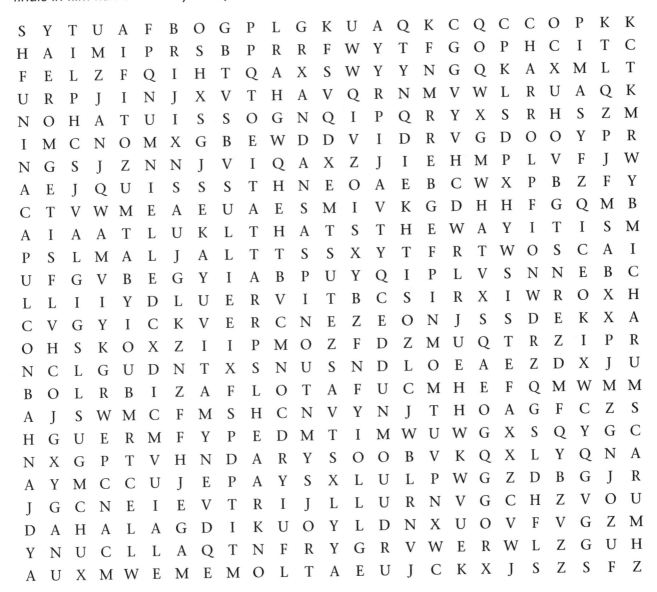

```
S Y T U A F B O G P L G K U A Q K C Q C C O P K K
H A I M I P R S B P R R F W Y T F G O P H C I T C
F E L Z F Q I H T Q A X S W Y Y N G Q K A X M L T
U R P J I N J X V T H A V Q R N M V W L R U A Q K
N O H A T U I S S O G N Q I P Q R Y X S R H S Z M
I M C N O M X G B E W D D V I D R V G D O O Y P R
N G S J Z N N J V I Q A X Z J I E H M P L V F J W
A E J Q U I S S S T H N E O A E B C W X P B Z F Y
C T V W M E A E U A E S M I V K G D H H F G M B B
A I A A T L U K L T H A T S T H E W A Y I T I S M
P S L M A L J A L T T S S X Y T R T W O S C A I
U F G V B E G Y I A B P U Y Q I P L V S N N E B C
L L I I Y D L U E R V I T B C S I R X I W R O X H
C V G Y I C K V E R C N E Z E O N J S S S D E K X A
O H S K O X Z I I P M O Z F D Z M U Q T R Z I P R
N C L G U D N T X S N U S N D L O E A E Z D X J U
B O L R B I Z A F L O T A F U C M H E F Q M W M M
A J S W M C F M S H C N V Y N J T H O A G F C Z S
H G U E R M F Y P E D M T I M W U W G X S Q Y G C
N X G P T V H N D A R Y S O O B V K Q X L Y Q N A
A Y M C C U J E P A Y S X L U L P W G Z D B G J R
J G C N E I E V T R I J L L U R N V G C H Z V O U
D A H A L A G D I K U O Y L D N X U O V F V G Z M
Y N U C L L A Q T N F R Y G R V W E R W L Z G U H
A U X M W E M E M O L T A E U J C K X J S Z S F Z
```

With actress Leticia Roman on the set of *G.I. Blues* in 1960.

More B Sides

This set of questions is a continuation of an earlier quiz. All of the B sides below reached the Top Forty. Name the A side of each.

1. "Anything That's Part of You" _____

2. "There Goes My Everything" _____

3. "I Gotta Know" _____

4. "My Baby Left Me" _____

5. "Playing for Keeps" _____

6. "His Latest Flame" _____

7. "Don't Ask Me Why" _____

8. "Treat Me Nice" _____

9. "It Hurts Me" _____

10. "Lonely Man" _____

11. "I Need Your Love Tonight" _____

12. "My Wish Came True" _____

13. "I Beg of You" _____

14. "Doncha' Think It's Time" _____

★ Elvis showed promise as a high school football player, but he complied with his mother's request that he quit playing because she was worried he would be injured.

Elvis and the Army

Rock & rollers may have been saddened to see Elvis inducted into the army, but their parents seemed to get some inner satisfaction from seeing that even the King of Rock & Roll would have to take time out to serve his country. Probably no other individual ever had his military duty examined more closely than did Elvis. It's been a long time, but see if you can pin down some of the facts relating to Elvis's short military career.

ACROSS

5. Method of transportation back to Memphis following Elvis's discharge
6. Relative who died while Elvis was in basic training
9. Elvis's rank upon discharge
10. The place where Elvis received his army indoctrination
12. First big hit following his 1960 discharge
13. Basic training site
14. Month Elvis was discharged
16. Month Elvis was drafted
17. Type of outfit in which Elvis served
18. Name of hospital where Elvis took preinduction army physical

DOWN

1. Texas town where Elvis lived during basic training
2. Vehicle associated with Elvis's army tour
3. Maiden name of Priscilla, whom Elvis met while in West Germany
4. Woman Vernon met in West Germany (while Elvis was in the army) and later married
7. Elvis received a temporary deferment so that he could finish work on this movie.
8. Famous entertainer with whom Elvis teamed for a television special following his discharge
11. The New Jersey location of Elvis's 1960 discharge
15. Rank of Priscilla's stepfather when Elvis asked permission for her to travel to Graceland
19. Network that aired Elvis's postarmy television special

★ In March 1955, Elvis, Scotty Moore, and Bill Black auditioned for the TV program "Arthur Godfrey's Talent Scouts," but they were turned down. In 1957, Buddy Holly and the Crickets met the same fate.

★ While in West Germany as a member of the U.S. Army, Elvis reportedly received from eight thousand to ten thousand letters a week.

Elvis's Biggest-Selling Hits

It is difficult to rank Elvis's biggest hits in exact order of sales. Elvis: His Life from A to Z *claims that "It's Now or Never" is his biggest seller with global sales of more than 22 million. This quiz uses these criteria: (1) Recording Industry Association of America (RIAA) certification; (2) Number of weeks at number one, as the first tie-breaker; and (3) Total number of weeks on the charts, as the second tie-breaker. All of the songs below were RIAA-certified platinum or multi-platinum. Rank his top ten hits in order. To make the quiz more interesting, there are five extras that are closely associated with Elvis, but aren't in his top ten.*

1. _____ "All Shook Up"

2. _____ "Are You Lonesome Tonight?"

3. _____ "Burning Love"

4. _____ "Can't Help Falling in Love"

5. _____ "Don't"

6. _____ "Don't Be Cruel/Hound Dog"

7. _____ "Heartbreak Hotel"

8. _____ "In the Ghetto"

9. _____ "It's Now or Never"

10. _____ "Jailhouse Rock"

11. _____ "Love Me Tender"

12. _____ "Return to Sender"

13. _____ "Stuck on You"

14. _____ "Suspicious Minds"

15. _____ "Teddy Bear"

★ In 1986, Elvis was selected as one of the charter members of the Rock and Roll Hall of Fame in Cleveland, Ohio.

★ Before Elvis began shooting *Love Me Tender*, he learned not only his own lines but also those of all the other actors and actresses in the film.

Loves of His Life

Although Elvis married only once, he met, dated, or was romantically linked with a number of beautiful women during his life. Sometimes these involvements proved to be only fleeting encounters, while some were more durable. Put those supermarket tabloids out of your mind and see how you are at remembering the facts.

_____ 1. Athlete and television personality who married Linda Thompson

_____ 2. High school girlfriend

_____ 3. Girlfriend who discovered Elvis dead at Graceland

_____ 4. Main girlfriend following his divorce

_____ 5. Karate instructor who stole Priscilla from the King

_____ 6. Introduced Elvis to his future wife

_____ 7. *Playboy* Playmate who dated Elvis before marrying actor James Caan

_____ 8. German teenager who dated Elvis while he was in West Germany

_____ 9. Actress girlfriend who later married actor Roger Smith

_____ 10. Claimed Elvis fathered her son

_____ 11. Priscilla's lover following her romance with the karate instructor

_____ 12. Former wife of Eddie Fisher who dated Elvis briefly in the early 1960s

_____ 13. Famous stripper who claimed to have had an affair with Elvis

A. Sheila Ryan

B. Tempest Storm

C. Currie Grant

D. Bruce Jenner

E. Michael Edwards

F. Ann-Margret

G. Dixie Locke

H. Connie Stevens

I. Mike Stone

J. Margrit Buergin

K. Linda Thompson

L. Ginger Alden

M. Patricia Ann Parker

★ **Red West, a bodyguard and member of the Memphis Mafia, wrote or cowrote several songs for Elvis, including "Separate Ways" and "If You Talk in Your Sleep."**

★ 43 Kent's Favorites

Because I have enjoyed so many Elvis songs, it is very difficult to limit my list of favorites to only ten. For the most part, I have chosen songs that were not big hits. They are not as well known as the songs on David's list, which appears earlier in this book. If you are familiar with the songs, compare your opinions of them with my descriptions. Better still, listen to them and see what you think. In any case, unscramble the titles.

1. An autobiographical song about a man experiencing divorce and trying to explain it as he says good-bye to his daughter. The sad, touching words are sung convincingly with sincerity and emotion.

   YAWS PAAREETS

   _____

2. One of Elvis's many beautiful religious songs. I remember hearing this ballad in a small country church when I was a boy. It is a sweet, simple song from a simpler, rural era and Elvis sings it tenderly. It speaks of Christians seeing friends in heaven. Some people consider the words to be syrupy, but I admit that I am incurably sentimental.

   TEME FI EW GINAA RENEV

   _____

3. This song is about an irresponsible husband who leaves his wife, finds out that freedom isn't what he thought it would be, and wants her back. Elvis is really good at singing songs like this that are serious and have a message about life in the real world.

   GIHTNS TTNEWY DAN NEWTTY YADS

   _____

4. Great lyrics, sung to perfection, with words rolling over his tongue and often broken up into several notes. A sad blues song about lost love that ends with a Slim Whitman-style high-note finish.

   FO A SUELB SEMS

   _____

5. Cute lyrics with a playful beat. The bass countermelody sung by the Jordanaires provides a gorgeous duet.

   TAGTO WOKN I

   _____

6. An upbeat, gutsy, country blues song about an incomparable former girlfriend. Turn up the volume and experience the mature depth of Elvis's voice.

   TAERF OYU VOINLG

   _____

7. I liked the lyrics when I first heard this song as a mellow ballad on the *Best of Eddy Arnold* album. But Elvis really gives the tune life and emotion, and breathes fire into it. It's country with soul—truly one of Elvis's best styles.

   OT 'TODN I TANW WOKN LEARYL

   _____

8. A sad ballad sung with sensitivity and beauty. Another heartbreaking song about lost love. (For some reason, sad songs usually pack a stronger punch.) Mellow verses with a fuller chorus. A nice piano background.

TARP FO TTAHS' UYO GAINNYTH   _____

9. The title track from Elvis's first full-length religious album. This is a beautiful hymn. Play this for your mother if she is skeptical about whether or not Elvis really could sing. The meaningful words are treated gently and reverently. The song includes Elvis singing a duet with himself, a captivating low-voiced verse solo, and a climactic conclusion.

NEIM SHI ANHD NI   _____

10. A plea to be reunited in love that surely no woman could resist. It is romantic with a slightly bouncy beat and was sung in the movie *Blue Hawaii*.

ROEM ON   _____

Elvis and costar Juliet Prowse admire three sets of twins on the set of *G.I. Blues.*

★ Contemporaries of the 1960s

After Elvis left the army, the hits just kept rolling on. Despite the one-way trip to oblivion taken by many rockers during the British Invasion of the early and mid-1960s, more than fifty of the King's songs cracked the Top Forty during the 1960s. Still, there was some great rock & roll during the sixties. See if you are able to complete the following crossword concerning Elvis's contemporaries of this decade.

ACROSS

1. A group of New Jersey girls who wondered if their boyfriend would love them tomorrow
4. He was running scared until he found a pretty woman in 1964 (first name).
5. He took his hat off to Larry but not on his biggest hit.
6. She said she was sorry in 1960, but she was still alone in 1962 (first name).
9. He didn't want to go with Mr. Custer.
11. In 1963 this group redid Johnny Mathis's big 1957 hit "Wonderful! Wonderful!"
12. A one-hit group that scored with the number-one "Green Tambourine" in 1968
14. They were groovin'.
15. It was her party (first name).
16. First it was mashed potatoes and later the gravy.
17. They sang about the leader of the pack.
18. Switched to the Warner label in 1960 and they cried in the rain but didn't "Walk Right Back"

DOWN

2. Last name of a father-daughter duo that had a number-one hit in 1967
3. His first big hit in 1960 concerned the movement of poetry.
7. Once a lead singer for the Drifters, he went solo with "Spanish Harlem."
8. Group led first by Curtis Mayfield and later by Jerry Butler
9. Babysitter of Carole King who had a number-one hit in 1962 with one of Carole's songs about a new dance
10. In 1962, after shooting Liberty Valence, love broke his heart.
13. He liked it like that.

★ Bill Medley, who was a member of the Righteous Brothers, was offered the song "In the Ghetto" before Elvis recorded it and made it a platinum record, but he turned it down.

★ During the late 1960s, Pat Boone often joined Elvis and other stars for touch football games.

Dear Elvis

Charlotte Moore, Kent's clever sister from Missouri, came up with the format for this quiz. Think of Elvis as an advice columnist like Dear Abby. Below are some letters to Elvis that are based on themes from a few of his more popular songs. How would he respond, using the titles of these songs to answer the questions that are posed? After you complete the quiz, how about dusting off your Elvis record collection and listening to the lyrics? Maybe the King has some words for you.

1. "My darling has made my life complete and I love her very much. She fulfills all of my dreams and I want to be with her forever. What should I ask her to do?"

   _____

2. "You can always find me at home by myself. I wish my baby would at least call me. I'm sorry if I said something that upset her. I really do love her, and she's the only girl I think about. I sure wish she would come see me and love me. What would you say to her?"

   _____

3. "My heart is restless and weary. I hear a dream calling me and I want someone to look for it with me. What should I do?"

   _____

4. "Our father cried a lot in bed last night, and this morning it seemed that he just wanted to give up. He wonders why we all have to go through so much pain and hurt. What can we say to comfort him?"

   _____

5. "I keep getting letters from my boyfriend. We had an argument, and I don't want to hear from him anymore. What should I do with the letters?"

   _____

6. "I love my darling so much that she holds the key to my life. For her, I'm willing to be strong, weak, tame, wild, foolish, or wise. If she would take me, she could mold my heart. What can I promise her to convince her how much I love her and how flexible I am?"

   _____

7. "When my baby and I kiss, our hearts are aflame. I want to hold her in the bright moonlight and make this magical night an evening of love. In a word, what should I ask her to do?"

   _____

8. "People say that my girlfriend and I are too young to go steady, but I know that our love is forever. What should I ask her to do to show the world that she's mine?"

_____

9. "I am particular about how my baby acts toward me. I want her to be polite, kiss me a lot, and scratch my back. What can I tell her about how I want her to behave?"

_____

10. "My darling is stingy with her affection and I'm hungry for lovin'. I don't mean to be greedy, but I do want some kisses—in fact, a lot of kisses—from her honey-filled beehive. What do you think she should give me?"

_____

Elvis signs autographs for Duke University football players in December 1960.

Top to bottom: Elvis with *Love Me Tender*'s Debra Paget (1956) and *Wild in the Country*'s Tuesday Weld (1961).

Leading Ladies

Elvis appeared with many beautiful women during the course of his thirteen-year movie career. See if you are able to match the King's leading ladies with the movies in which they appeared.

_____ 1. Ursula Andress	A. *Blue Hawaii*
_____ 2. Joan Blackman	B. *Change of Habit*
_____ 3. Donna Douglas	C. *Frankie and Johnny*
_____ 4. Shelley Fabares	D. *Fun in Acapulco*
_____ 5. Carolyn Jones	E. *G.I. Blues*
_____ 6. Suzanna Leigh	F. *Girl Happy*
_____ 7. Ann-Margret	G. *Girls! Girls! Girls!*
_____ 8. Mary Ann Mobley	H. *Harum Scarum*
_____ 9. Mary Tyler Moore	I. *It Happened at the World's Fair*
_____ 10. Joan O'Brien	J. *King Creole*
_____ 11. Juliet Prowse	K. *Loving You*
_____ 12. Lizabeth Scott	L. *Paradise, Hawaiian Style*
_____ 13. Nancy Sinatra	M. *Speedway*
_____ 14. Stella Stevens	N. *Viva Las Vegas*
_____ 15. Tuesday Weld	O. *Wild in the Country*

Bonus Question: Name two additional Elvis movies not listed above in which Shelley Fabares starred.

★ **Elvis was offered several movie parts that did not work out, often because of Colonel Parker's unyielding demands. Among these were the role of a gang member in *West Side Story*, the role played by Tony Curtis in *The Defiant Ones*, and the starring role opposite Barbra Streisand in *A Star Is Born*.**

★ Money Matters

Despite the fact that Elvis earned tens of millions of dollars for himself and others, he remained relatively unsophisticated about handling money. Perhaps the best example of his naïveté is that he appointed his father, a man with an eighth grade education, as his business manager. See how much you know about Elvis's financial affairs.

_____ 1. The approximate price at which RCA purchased Elvis's contract from Sun Records

    A. $5,000   D. $1 million
    B. $35,000   E. $5 million
    C. $500,000

_____ 2. How much Elvis's parents paid for his first guitar

    A. $3.95   D. $25.00
    B. $7.75   E. $39.95
    C. $18.50

_____ 3. Elvis's approximate monthly salary upon induction into the U.S. Army

    A. $25   D. $155
    B. $50   E. $350
    C. $80

_____ 4. What Elvis bought his mother with his 1955 bonus from RCA

    A. Cadillac   D. trip to Europe
    B. Lincoln   E. pacemaker
    C. new home

_____ 5. Elvis's salary for acting in *Love Me Tender*

    A. $10,000   D. $500,000
    B. $50,000   E. $1 million
    C. $100,000

_____ 6. Nightly pay to Elvis for his initial appearances on "The Louisiana Hayride"

    A. $6   D. $100
    B. $18   E. $250
    C. $50

_____ 7. The largest portion of Elvis's income ever collected by the Colonel for acting as manager and agent

    A. 6 percent   D. 33 percent
    B. 10 percent   E. 50 percent
    C. 20 percent

8. *Forbes* magazine's estimate of the 1987 income generated by Elvis and his music (royalties, Graceland visitation, etc.) ten years after his death

   A. $1 million
   B. $5 million
   C. $10 million

   D. $15 million
   E. $50 million

9. The price Elvis paid for his jet, *Lisa Marie*

   A. $500,000
   B. $900,000
   C. $1.2 million

   D. $2.5 million
   E. $5 million

10. Total payment for three appearances on "The Ed Sullivan Show"

    A. $5,000
    B. $25,000
    C. $50,000

    D. $100,000
    E. $1 million

11. Approximate price that Elvis paid for Graceland

    A. $102,500
    B. $238,500
    C. $524,800

    D. $1.3 million
    E. $3.4 million

12. The Internal Revenue Service claim for back taxes following Elvis's death

    A. $5 million
    B. $10 million
    C. $50 million

    D. $250 million
    E. $1.25 billion

13. Vernon Presley's approximate weekly income as a laborer after the family moved to Memphis

    A. $25.00
    B. $38.50
    C. $50.00

    D. $75.00
    E. $100.00

★ Elvis's last will and testament was witnessed by Ginger Alden (a girlfriend), Charles Hodge (an aide), and Ann Dewey Smith (the wife of Elvis's attorney).

★ Number-One Songs by Contemporaries of Elvis

48

It is interesting to place Elvis's songs in the context of other songs that were popular at the same time. This quiz deals with songs that were number one immediately preceding or following an Elvis number-one hit. Name the songs that are being described.

1. "Heavenly" song by Shelley Fabares that preceded "Good Luck Charm" at the top of the charts in the spring of 1962.

   _____

2. Song by the Browns that "rang in" at the top in mid-1959 following the King's "A Big Hunk o' Love."

   _____

3. "Intoxicating" instrumental by the Champs that followed "Don't" in early 1958.

   _____

4. First of two number-one songs by Guy Mitchell, this tune was also recorded by Marty Robbins. First hitting number one at the end of 1956, it immediately preceded "Too Much."

   _____

5. Song by Gogi Grant about restless, wandering hearts that caused "Heartbreak Hotel" to check out of number one in June 1956.

   _____

6. A request by Maurice Williams and the Zodiacs for you to hang around a while. It came before "Are You Lonesome Tonight?" in late 1960.

   _____

7. Meditative plea by the Platters that came between "I Want You, I Need You, I Love You" and "Don't Be Cruel" in August 1956.

   _____

8. Instrumental movie theme by Percy Faith that preceded "Stuck on You" in early 1960.

   _____

9. Comedy, novelty song by Sheb Wooley about a strange creature. It was replaced by "Hard Headed Woman" in mid-1958.

   _____

10. In his only number-one song, Sam Cooke was "moved" by his girlfriend. The song moved "Jail-house Rock" out of the top slot in late 1957.

_____

11. Song by Pat Boone about an unusual type of communication. It came between "All Shook Up" and "Teddy Bear" in mid-1957.

_____

12. Temptations hit that was "next to" (just before) "Suspicious Minds" in late 1969.

_____

13. A song by Brian Hyland about skimpy female apparel. It was removed from the top spot by "It's Now or Never" in mid-1960.

_____

14. Written in the 1930s and recorded on an album by Elvis in the 1950s, this ding-a-dong-ding Marcels tune caused "Surrender" to surrender the number-one position in the spring of 1961. This was one wild song!

_____

15. Song about youthful romance that was a hit for both Tab Hunter and Sonny James. Tab's version was too much for Elvis and bumped "Too Much" from the number-one slot in early 1957.

_____

16. Song by the Shirelles that also appeared on an Elvis album at a very appropriate time—right after the King's return from the army. It replaced "Good Luck Charm" at the top.

_____

17. Perry Como had people going in circles in 1957 with this hit that preceded "All Shook Up."

_____

18. Chubby Checker had a good time "horsing around" with this 1961 hit that waved the white flag to "Surrender."

_____

19. The Everly Brothers' girlfriend went to sleep during this 1957 predecessor to "Jailhouse Rock."

_____

20. Bert Kaempfert instrumental with a title concerning the wonders of evening that displaced "Are You Lonesome Tonight?" in 1961. Bert was one of the writers of "Wooden Heart."

_____

Bonus Question: What two 1956 Elvis singles topped the charts back to back? (Hint: One had a flip side about an animal, and the other was a ballad title tune from a movie.)

49

Elvis Potpourri

To keep your mind agile, here's a crossword that includes questions concerning a variety of subjects regarding the King of Rock & Roll. Music, people, places, and events are all covered in this potpourri crossword.

ACROSS

1. Elvis's first gold single
4. The hotel where Elvis and Priscilla were married
5. Country in which the Colonel was born
7. Color of the Cadillac Elvis bought for his mother
8. Memphis hospital where Elvis was taken at his death
10. One of Elvis's most noticeable features
12. Where Elvis and his mother were entombed before being moved to Graceland
13. Early Elvis manager
14. Comedian on whose television show Elvis appeared twice in 1956
15. Group that named Elvis one of the "Ten Outstanding Young Men of America" in 1971
16. Elvis's last gold single
17. Priscilla's nighttime TV soap opera

DOWN

2. Show on which Elvis made his first television appearance
3. Tupelo junior high school Elvis attended
6. One of the King's favorite sports
9. Recorded "The King Is Gone" after Elvis's death
11. Wink Martindale's television show on which Elvis appeared in 1956

The star and six-year-old Dicky Tiu receive dialogue instructions in 1962 on the set of *It Happened at the World's Fair.*

★50 Elvis CDs Keep on Comin'

RCA Records searched its vaults and found many new Elvis recordings. As a result, RCA has released a steady stream of more than fifty CDs/albums and multi-CD sets since Elvis left us in 1977. (LP albums were discontinued in late 1990.) Match the sample of eighteen CD/LP titles with their descriptions.

_____ 1. *Amazing Grace*

_____ 2. *Collector's Gold*

_____ 3. *Command Performances: Essential '60s Masters II*

_____ 4. *Double Features*

_____ 5. *Elvis: A Legendary Performer, Volume 3*

_____ 6. *Elvis Aron Presley*

_____ 7. *Essential Elvis*

_____ 8. *From Nashville to Memphis: Essential '60s Masters I*

_____ 9. *A Golden Celebration*

_____ 10. *The King of Rock & Roll: The Complete '50s Masters*

_____ 11. *The Memphis Record*

_____ 12. *Platinum: A Life in Music*

_____ 13. *Reconsider Baby*

_____ 14. *Return of the Rocker*

_____ 15. *Rhythm & Country*

_____ 16. *This Is Elvis*

_____ 17. *A Valentine Gift for You*

_____ 18. *Walk a Mile in My Shoes: Essential '70s Masters*

A. 1978 picture disk

B. 1980 eight-LP set to commemorate the twenty-fifth anniversary of Elvis's signing with RCA

C. Soundtrack for 1981 documentary

D. 1984 six-LP set with all performances on the Ed Sullivan, Steve Allen, Milton Berle, and Dorsey Brothers shows; rereleased as a four-CD set in 1998

E. Red vinyl LP of love songs to celebrate Elvis's fiftieth birthday

F. 1985 collection of rhythm and blues songs

G. 1986 release of early '60s soft rock songs

H. Must-have 1987 CD from the acclaimed 1969 American Studios sessions

I. Series of CDs of alternate takes, beginning in 1988

J. 1991 three-CD set of alternate takes from movies, studio recordings, and live performances

K. 1992 five-CD set of all songs from the decade; called "monumental" and given a five-star rating by *Rolling Stone*

L. 1993 five-CD set that was Elvis's 111th gold record

M. 1993–1995 series of nine CDs with all songs recorded for twenty movies

N. 1995 two-CD set with sixty-two of the best '60s movie songs

O. 1994 two-CD set of fifty-five gospel recordings

P. 1995 five-CD set of best songs from Elvis's last decade

Q. 1997 four-CD set with seventy-seven unreleased performances

R. 1998 CD of alternate takes from the 1973 Stax Studios sessions

★ **Elvis was inducted into the Country Music Hall of Fame in 1998.**

★ **The Elvis stamp issued in 1993 was by far the most profitable U.S. postage stamp in history. More than 500 million were sold, resulting in a profit of $36 million, because many of the stamps were purchased as collector's items and never used.**

The rocker and the actor.

Order on the Tube

It's not hard to figure out that Elvis appeared on "The Ed Sullivan Show" before he did his worldwide "Aloha from Hawaii" special. That's like saying that he recorded "Hound Dog" before he waxed "Suspicious Minds." Ah, but did the King appear with Milton Berle before he did his first show with Ed Sullivan? Now that's the nitty-gritty kind of question that should appeal to the real Elvis fan. See if you can make some order out of the following list of television appearances. Number them from one to ten, in chronological order.

_____ A. Elvis appears on ABC's "Frank Sinatra-Timex Special."

_____ B. The King makes his last appearance on "The Ed Sullivan Show."

_____ C. Elvis is interviewed on "Dance Party" by Wink Martindale.

_____ D. Elvis appears on "The Steve Allen Show."

_____ E. Elvis makes his first appearance on "The Louisiana Hayride."

_____ F. Worldwide broadcast of "Elvis: Aloha from Hawaii."

_____ G. The Singer Corporation-sponsored "Elvis" appears on NBC.

_____ H. Elvis makes his first appearance on "The Milton Berle Show."

_____ I. The King makes his first appearance on Tommy and Jimmy Dorsey's "Stage Show."

_____ J. Elvis is interviewed via telephone by Dick Clark on "American Bandstand."

★ **Sammy Davis, Jr., appeared with Elvis on the "Frank Sinatra-Timex Special" TV program and is shown as a member of the audience in the movie *Elvis—That's the Way It Is*.**

★ **When the movie *Elvis* was shown on ABC-TV in February 1979, it had higher ratings than either of the other heavyweight movies shown in the same time slot, *Gone with the Wind* and *One Flew over the Cuckoo's Nest*.**

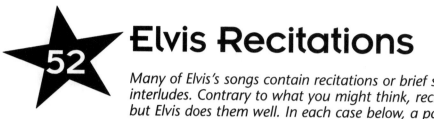

Elvis Recitations

Many of Elvis's songs contain recitations or brief speaking parts as introductions or interludes. Contrary to what you might think, recitations are not easy to do effectively, but Elvis does them well. In each case below, a paraphrase of the recitation or speaking portion is given, along with an additional clue. Name the songs from which they came.

1. "I wonder if you feel alone. Each of us is playing a role in life and you were my darling. When we first met, you read your lines well, but in the second act, you changed and I don't understand why. I trusted you, but you lied about loving me. I'm so empty that I can't live without you and I'm ready for the curtain to come down on my life." (Probably Elvis's most famous recitation.)

   _____

2. "When you see your darling in a friend's arms, your hurt will start. Love cannot be shared." (A popular song in its own right, it is the flip side of a monster hit from the fifties.)

   _____

3. "When I awoke, all I saw were four drab walls around me." (This song was originally a country hit. Later, it was a pop hit by Tom Jones before being recorded by Elvis on an album in the 1970s.)

   _____

4. "I kept a Bible with a rose inside it that my mother had saved. The rose found a hiding place between the pages." (The B side of a 1970 Top Ten hit.)

   _____

5. "Do you really mean it when you say you love me?" (Appeared on a 1973 album; released as a single after Elvis's death.)

   _____

6. "Sweetheart, I'm wounded more than you will ever realize because I'm still in love with you." (A Top Thirty hit late in Elvis's career.)

   _____

7. "Through the years, I'll be glad to share your joys and tears. Just ask for help when things go wrong and I'll come." (The recitation did not appear on the 1965 Top Twenty single version of this song; instrumentation was substituted. It did, however, appear on the 1962 album version.)

   _____

8. "Some of you have never spent much time in the South, so I'll tell you a story. A plant grows down there and that's all some people have to eat, but they get along OK." (Never released as a single but frequently done by Elvis in concert during the 1970s.)

_____

9. "I can recall my first love relationship—it went completely wrong. My mother gave me some advice and I can still hear those words. So I put them in this song." (A rhythm & blues song that was a Top Ten hit for a soul singer in 1969 and was recorded by Elvis soon afterward.)

_____

10. "I will say good-bye gently. I would be heartbroken if you saw me leave. So I'll be gone before you realize it, and before you plead for me not to go, and before tears start to fall." (This very touching song deals with a man who doesn't want to wake his wife to tell her he is dying. Elvis did it in concert, and it was released after his death.)

_____

A charitable Elvis donates FDR's former yacht to St. Jude Hospital while Danny Thomas looks on.

⭐ **53** Perplexing Song Titles

Here is another set of questions about the King's music. If you are really a fan, you will eat this one up. If you don't do so well, pull some Elvis records out of your collection, look at the covers or jackets closely, and then try again. Complete this crossword by coming up with the song titles hinted at below.

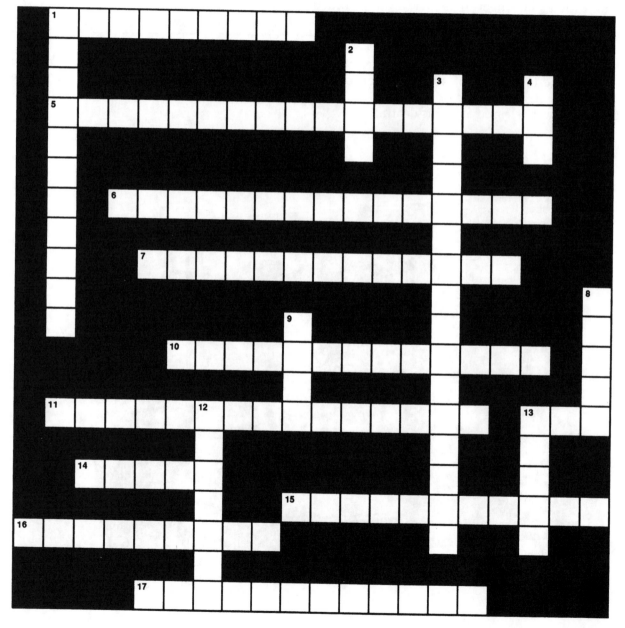

ACROSS
1. "Put Your Hand ____"
5. Elvis's biggest religious single
6. Longest single recorded by Elvis
7. "Bridge over ____"
10. Elvis's first religious album
11. "Clean Up ____"
13. "Tell Me ____"
14. First single released after Elvis's death
15. Elvis sings in German in this song
16. "Walk a Mile ____"
17. Elvis's first single of the 1970s

DOWN
1. Last song in Elvis's 1968 TV special
2. Elvis Christmas recording: "The First ____"
3. No one is as pretty as "____"
4. "Flip, Flop, and ____"
8. "If ____ Day Was Like Christmas"
9. "That's All Right, ____"
12. Last single before Elvis's death
13. "I Got a ____"

Viva Las Vegas costar Ann-Margret meets Elvis for the first time in 1963.

The King and the Prez in their famous White House rendezvous on December 21, 1970.

★ Before joining Elvis's band as lead guitarist, James Burton played lead guitar for Ricky Nelson on many of the Travelin' Man's hits, including "Poor Little Fool."

Names of Movie Characters

This is an extra challenge for Elvis movie buffs. Match the movie title with the name of the character that Elvis played in the film. This quiz is a tough one.

_____	1. *Blue Hawaii*	A. Lonnie Beale
_____	2. *Change of Habit*	B. Pacer Burton
_____	3. *Flaming Star*	C. John Carpenter
_____	4. *Follow That Dream*	D. Ross Carpenter
_____	5. *Fun in Acapulco*	E. Mike Edwards
_____	6. *G.I. Blues*	F. Vince Everett
_____	7. *Girl Happy*	G. Danny Fisher
_____	8. *Girls! Girls! Girls!*	H. Chad Gates
_____	9. *It Happened at the World's Fair*	I. Walter Gulick
_____	10. *Jailhouse Rock*	J. Lucky Jackson
_____	11. *Kid Galahad*	K. Toby Kwimper
_____	12. *King Creole*	L. Mike McCoy
_____	13. *Kissin' Cousins*	M. Tulsa McLean
_____	14. *Love Me Tender*	N. Josh Morgan
_____	15. *Loving You*	O. Clint Reno
_____	16. *Roustabout*	P. Deke Rivers
_____	17. *Spinout*	Q. Charlie Rogers
_____	18. *Tickle Me*	R. Glenn Tyler
_____	19. *Viva Las Vegas*	S. Rusty Wells
_____	20. *Wild in the Country*	T. Mike Windgren

Bonus Question: In which of the above movies did Elvis also play a second character, Jodie Tatum?

★ **In 1971, Elvis received the Bing Crosby Award (later renamed the Lifetime Achievement Award) from the National Academy of Recording Arts and Sciences, in recognition of his musical creativity and influence.**

Elvis Dos and Don'ts

Don't do this quiz! (Just kidding.) Actually, this quiz deals with song titles that include the word do *or the word* don't.

1. "Don't _ _ _ _ _ _ _ _ _ _ _ _"   A hit for Peter, Paul and Mary

2. "Don't _ _ _ _ _ _ _ _ _"   Flip side of "Hard Headed Woman"

3. "_ _ _ _ _ _ _ _ Don't   1970 country-flavored hit
   _ _ _ _ _ _ _ _ _ _"

4. "_ _ _ Don't _ _ _ _ _ _ _"   Ray Charles hit

5. "Do _ _ _ _ _ _ _"   Dance number from *Girl Happy*

6. "Don't _ _ _ _ _ _ _"   Multimillion seller

7. "Don't _ _ _ _ _ _ _ _ _"   Sentimental 1969 hit

8. "_ _ _ _ _ _ Don't _ _ _ _ _ _ _ _ _ _   Flip side of "Devil in Disguise"
   _ _ _ _ _ _ _ _ _ _ _ _ _"

9. "_ _ _ _ _ _ _ _ _ _ _ _ Don't   Sung in *Viva Las Vegas*
   _ _ _ _ _ _ _"

10. "Doncha' _ _ _ _ _ _ _ _ _ _ _ _ _ _"   Flip side of "Wear My Ring Around
                                                        Your Neck"

11. "Do _ _ _ _ _ _ _ _ _ _ _ _"   Don't bother me

12. "_ Don't _ _ _ _ _ _ _ _ _ _ _ _ _   1955 country rock song
    Don't _ _ _ _ _ _" (a double don't!)

13. "Don't _ _ _ _ _ _ _ _ _ _ _"   Sung in *Jailhouse Rock*

14. "_ Don't _ _ _ _ _ _ _"   Sung in *Girl Happy*

15. "_ _ _ _ _ Don't _ _ _ _ _ _ _ _ _"   From the *Raised on Rock* album

16. "_ Don't _ _ _ _ _ _ _ _ _ _ _ _"   Also from *Girl Happy*

17. "Do _ _ _ _ _ _ _"   1969 dance song

92

18. "_ _ _ Don't _ _ _ _ _ _ _ _ _

_ _ _ _ _ _ _ _ _"   1970 Top Twenty hit

19. "_ _ _ _ _ _ Don't _ _ _ _

_ _ _ _ _ _ _ _"   Flip side of "Frankie and Johnny"

20. "_ _ _ _"   A one-word title containing the
                                        word *don't*. This question should
                                        partly make up for the more
                                        difficult questions in this quiz.

 Probably no one knows exactly how many Elvis records have been sold, but RCA claims to have sold more than one billion—the equivalent of a thousand Gold Records.

★ Elvis won second prize at the Mississippi-Alabama Fair and Dairy show when he was ten years old for singing "Old Shep." He recorded the song eleven years later.

Backup Groups

Elvis was one of the first singers to make extensive use of background vocalists. Of course, the Jordanaires were his most famous backup group, but many other singers provided background for his records and concerts at various times during his career. Match the backup group with the description of what or when they performed.

_____ 1. Sang background from 1966 to 1971, including the *How Great Thou Art* album and the singles "I've Lost You" and "Until It's Time for You to Go"

_____ 2. Sang on the *It Happened at the World's Fair* sound track

_____ 3. Members of a gospel group that sang on "Heartbreak Hotel" and "I Want You, I Need You, I Love You," along with Gordon Stoker of the Jordanaires

_____ 4. High soprano who sang in 1970–1977 concerts

_____ 5. Also sang in 1970–1977 concerts; sang with Aretha Franklin at one time

_____ 6. Overdubbed vocal backing for "Tomorrow Night" in 1965; the song was originally recorded in 1955

_____ 7. Performed on the 1968 NBC-TV special

_____ 8. Sang on the "Do the Clam" single

_____ 9. Sang on the 1957 Christmas album, as well as in the Las Vegas concerts of the late sixties and the seventies

_____ 10. Sang on the 1975 *Today* album

_____ 11. Provided background for such diverse singles as "All Shook Up," "I Got Stung," "It's Now or Never," "Surrender," "Crying in the Chapel," "Viva Las Vegas," and "U.S. Male"

_____ 12. Sang in 1972–1977 concerts and on "Burning Love" and "Way Down"

_____ 13. Sang, along with the Jordanaires, on the *Fun in Acapulco* sound track

_____ 14. Sang on the "What'd I Say" single

_____ 15. Sang on the *Love Me Tender* sound track

★ **Between his high school graduation and the beginning of his recording career, Elvis drove a truck for Crown Electric Company in Memphis.**

A. The Amigos

B. The Anita Kerr Singers

C. The Blossoms

D. The Ken Darby Trio

E. The Imperials

F. The Jordanaires

G. The Jubliee Four and Carol Lombard Trio (two groups)

H. The Jubilee Four and Carol Lombard Quartet (two groups)

I. Millie Kirkham

J. The Mello Men

K. Ben and Brock Speer

L. The Stamps Quartet

M. The Sweet Inspirations

N. The Voice and the Holladays (two groups)

O. Kathy Westmoreland

★ **The Sweet Inspirations, one of Elvis's vocal backup groups, joined up with Rick Nelson following the King's death.**

The King during his acclaimed 1973 Aloha from Hawaii concert, which was beamed live worldwide via satellite.

Arrival in Charleston, West Virginia, in 1975 for three concerts.

Incorrect Titles

A friend of ours named Bob Otto likes to spell his name backward. Perhaps this is the reason that he tends to remember the titles of Elvis's songs and movies in an opposite or confused manner. For example, the song he calls "You're Mine" is really "I'm Yours." Get the idea? See if you can correct the titles below that Bob has come up with.

1. "Big Brother" _____

2. "You've Found Me" _____

3. "A Small Bit of Hate" _____

4. *Tame in the Big City* _____

5. "Banjo Woman" _____

6. "Hug Me Slowly" _____

7. "Such a Difficult Answer" _____

8. *Green Alaska* _____

9. "Foreign Female" _____

10. "Don't Laugh, Mama" _____

11. "Tennessee Snow" _____

12. *Stay Here, Jane* _____

13. "Your Girl" _____

14. *Unaffectionate Relatives* _____

15. "Run Away from That Nightmare" _____

16. "All Calmed Down" _____

17. "A Wise Person Such as You" _____

18. *Fishfry* _____

19. "Not Enough" _____

20. "Don't Give Up" _____

58 ★ Songs Sung, But Not Officially Recorded, by Elvis

The songs listed below were sung in concert one or more times by Elvis, but were not officially released during his lifetime. Some of them have appeared on bootleg albums, and RCA has released a few of them posthumously. In yet another testimonial to Elvis's versatility, the hit versions of these songs were done by twenty different artists. Match the song title with the artist who recorded it.

_____ 1. "Blowin' in the Wind"

_____ 2. "The Cattle Call"

_____ 3. "Chain Gang"

_____ 4. "Close to You"

_____ 5. "Diana"

_____ 6. "Fools Hall of Fame"

_____ 7. "Gone"

_____ 8. "The Great Pretender"

_____ 9. "House of the Rising Sun"

_____ 10. "I Can See Clearly Now"

_____ 11. "I Walk the Line"

_____ 12. "I Write the Songs"

_____ 13. "I'm Leaving It Up to You"

_____ 14. "Jambalaya (On the Bayou)"

_____ 15. "Mr. Tambourine Man"

_____ 16. "My Woman, My Woman, My Wife"

_____ 17. "Rock Around the Clock"

_____ 18. "Roses Are Red"

_____ 19. "The Twelfth of Never"

_____ 20. "You Can Have Her"

A. The Animals

B. Paul Anka

C. Eddy Arnold

D. Pat Boone

E. The Byrds

F. The Carpenters

G. Johnny Cash

H. Sam Cooke

I. Dale and Grace

J. Fats Domino

K. Bill Haley and His Comets

L. Roy Hamilton

M. Ferlin Husky

N. Barry Manilow

O. Johnny Mathis

P. Johnny Nash

Q. Peter, Paul and Mary

R. The Platters

S. Marty Robbins

T. Bobby Vinton

Friends of the King

In his short life Elvis came into contact with a large number and wide variety of individuals. Many were well known in their own right, but an even larger number were relatively ordinary people who would be known only by true fans of Elvis. See if you can match the person with the relationship.

_____ 1. Minnie Mae Hood

_____ 2. Marvin Gambill, Jr.

_____ 3. Bernie Baum

_____ 4. Marian Cocke

_____ 5. Wink Martindale

_____ 6. Mike Stone

_____ 7. Rita Moreno

_____ 8. Bob Moore

_____ 9. Jerry Schilling

_____ 10. Nancy Rooks

_____ 11. Sheila Ryan

_____ 12. Ed Hill

_____ 13. Lou Wright

_____ 14. D. J. Fontana

_____ 15. Joe Esposito

_____ 16. Elsie Marmann

_____ 17. Jimmy Ellis

_____ 18. Pat Biggs

_____ 19. Ann Beaulieu

_____ 20. Max Baer, Jr.

A. Elvis's girlfriend after Linda Thompson

B. Personal valet and chauffeur of Elvis

C. Singer with a voice much like the King's

D. Member of a songwriting team that wrote many Elvis songs

E. Member of the Stamps Quartet

F. Priscilla Presley's mother

G. Longtime Elvis bodyguard

H. Main aide and close friend of the King

I. Priscilla's karate instructor and, later, her lover

J. Replaced Bill Black as bass player during recording sessions

K. Television star who was a close friend of Elvis

L. Longtime drummer for Elvis

M. Vernon Presley's brother-in-law

N. Memphis television personality who interviewed Elvis early in the King's career

O. Elvis's high school music teacher

P. Psychic for Elvis

Q. Graceland cook who coauthored cookbook with Vernon

R. Maiden name of Elvis's paternal grandmother

S. Famous dancer who briefly dated Elvis

T. Personal nurse to Elvis during mid-1970s

⭐60 More Letters to Elvis

The romance of male-female relationships must be important. At least, most of Elvis's songs seem to dwell upon this topic. Again, these letters are based on the text of Elvis's songs. Using his song titles, how would he answer those who are seeking his advice? Since these songs are not so well known, we have provided the titles in scrambled form.

1. "My girlfriend is nearby, and I would like to hug her a little and let her know my true feelings. I would like to empty my heart, but on the other hand I don't want her to know that I'm sad. I think I'll have a friend speak to her. What should he say? Sincerely, Jim."

   LELT MJI ERH LELHO DAIS TUSJ _____

2. "I tried to warn my friend that his new woman wouldn't be true, but he wouldn't listen and she broke his heart. I'm sorry about his troubles, but I'm tired of hearing about them. What should I tell him?"

   YBBA UYO TI 'SIT ROUY CORK _____

3. "Our love is unraveling, just falling apart. Indifference is a problem, but I would like to keep trying to rekindle our relationship. What should we do?"

   TI PU CHATP _____

4. "I know a man who is always criticizing and judging others. Yet, at the same time, he drinks excessively and cheats on his wife. What advice should I give him?"

   CAKB PU LNAEC DARY NOW ROUY _____

5. "A friend of mine is going to marry the only woman I ever loved. I want her to be happy but I can't bear to go to the wedding. What message should I send my friend?"

   DOGO FO KEAT REH RACE _____

6. "I'm in a romantic mood. I want to be kissed and hugged and have my hair messed up. I'm getting a little tired of waiting and wonder what I should say to my baby."

   KINHT SIT' CHADON' MITE _____

7. "My baby says she loves me, has brand-new kisses for me, and wants to hold me tight. Seeing is believing, and I think that it's time for her to prove to me that she cares. What should I tell her to let her know that she needs to demonstrate her love?"

   EM IT KAME NOKW _____

8. "My baby goes to college and drives a Cadillac. But I don't want her to be foolish and go with another man. I want her to return and be with me all the time like she used to be. What should I tell her in order to express my true intentions?"

   TELS' LAPY YABB SOUHE _____

9. "The one I loved has no heart and doesn't realize how much she has hurt me. She left me, and our home is gloomy and quiet. Life is hopeless, and I wish I could die. How do you think my friends refer to me now?"

EM LACL SEOOMNLE TUSJ _____

10. "I like to run wild, have fun, and stay on the move. I want to continue to be free and keep the girls guessing. How can I do it?"

EYS AYS REENV _____

The famous gates of Graceland, which feature the opening notes to "Love Me Tender."

More Word Pictures

You've done this before, but you'll have to admit it's great fun. Plus, it's probably a little easier than most things we have been throwing at you. See if you can determine the song titles being described by the pictures and clues below.

1.

_____

2.

_____

3.

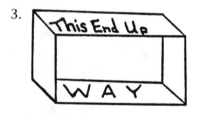

Elvis's last single before August 1977

4.

1967 single from the movie *Double Trouble*

5.

_____

6.

_____

_____

7.

Flip side of the 1975 single "Bringing It Back"

8.

Top Twenty single in 1965

9.

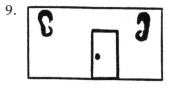

Sung in the movie *Girls! Girls! Girls!*

10.

_____

11.

12.

_____

Sung as a lullaby in *G.I. Blues*

13.

_____

14.

_____

15. it's night

_____

Flip side of "Promised Land"

Singles and Albums

The marketing of singles and albums has changed through the years. In the early days, the recording industry revolved around hit singles, and albums containing these singles were released after the singles had achieved prominence. Today, albums usually come first, and singles are selected from the albums for release. Following the pattern of the music industry, some Elvis hit singles appeared first as singles and others appeared first on albums. In any case, match each single below with the album that contained it.

_____	1. "Ask Me"	A.	*Clambake*
_____	2. "Crying in the Chapel"	B.	*Elvis: Aloha from Hawaii*
_____	3. "Guitar Man"	C.	*Elvis Country*
_____	4. "I Feel So Bad"	D.	*Elvis' Gold Records, Volume 2*
_____	5. "I Got Stung"	E.	*Elvis' Gold Records, Volume 4*
_____	6. "I Really Don't Want to Know"	F.	*Elvis' Golden Records*
_____	7. "If You Talk in Your Sleep"	G.	*Elvis' Golden Records, Volume 3*
_____	8. "I'm Yours"	H.	*Elvis—TV Special*
_____	9. "I've Got A Thing About You Baby"	I.	*Good Times*
_____	10. "Kentucky Rain"	J.	*How Great Thou Art*
_____	11. "Memories"	K.	*Pot Luck*
_____	12. "Steamroller Blues"	L.	*Promised Land*
_____	13. "There's Always Me"	M.	*Pure Gold*
_____	14. "Too Much"	N.	*Something for Everybody*
_____	15. "T-R-O-U-B-L-E"	O.	*That's the Way It Is*
_____	16. "You Don't Have to Say You Love Me"	P.	*Today*

★ **Elvis sang "Hound Dog," "Don't Be Cruel," and "Love Me Tender" on each of his three appearances on "The Ed Sullivan Show."**

Contemporaries of the 1970s

Elvis rolled into the seventies with renewed strength. He began touring again in February 1970 and continued a rigorous concert pace all the way through the summer of 1977, racking up another twenty-one Top Forty hits (including the number-two "Burning Love"). Most of the singers against which he had competed for chart positions during prior decades were long gone from the public spotlight, and the King had to prevail against an entirely new group of entertainers. See what you know about the rock & roll of a more modern era.

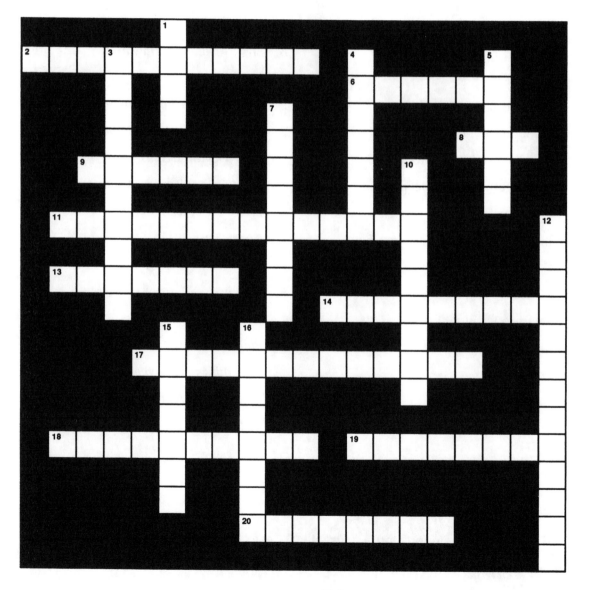

ACROSS

2. Group led by Wayne Fontana that had a big hit with "Game of Love"
6. Big group that included Don Henley and Glenn Frey
8. Raunchy and durable English rocker who wanted to know if you thought he was sexy (first name)
9. Had a big hit during the fifties with Mickey before going solo and hitting the Top Ten with "Pillow Talk" in 1973
11. Famous performer who had a number-one hit in 1970 that some thought was a takeoff on a Chiffons hit
13. Was really fond of Mandy (last name)
14. Former member of a major duo who had a solo hit about ways to leave your lover
17. Member of the sixties group, the Stone Poneys, who went solo and dated the governor of California
18. Member of the Beatles who redid a big 1960 hit by Johnny Burnette
19. Singer-songwriter who didn't want his girl-friend to get hooked on him
20. Had a number-one solo smash on the day Elvis died

DOWN

1. Former Memphis DJ who had a major 1976 hit about a dancing duck (last name)
3. Daughter of the King's chief 1950s competition; had a giant hit in the 1970s
4. Group of three brothers that battered the charts during the late 1970s
5. Member of musical family who redid a Paul Anka tune and had TV series with sister (last name)
7. Sang a song about Leroy Brown
10. Did a great (and long) song about the death of Buddy Holly
12. Lead singer of the Lovin' Spoonful who did a TV theme song that became a number-one hit
15. His song was sung blue in 1972 (last name)
16. Had many hits in the late fifties and then returned in the seventies with a song about having his baby

★ Kolya Vasin, a Soviet citizen who left his country for the first time in 1989 to visit Graceland, said "I listen to 'Jailhouse Rock' for the first time in 1958. After this shocking moment, I love Elvis forever." Mr. Vasin was wearing a black Elvis T-shirt and blue suede shoes when he stepped off the plane in Memphis.

More Big Hits by Elvis's Contemporaries

This quiz contains songs that were number one immediately before or after an Elvis song hit number one. In addition, there are several songs that were in the Top Five concurrently with songs by Elvis, but that did not reach number one. Name the songs being described.

1. Song by Paul Anka about a lonesome guy. Was followed by "A Big Hunk o' Love" in 1959.

   _____

2. Song by Danny and the Juniors about being at a dance. Preceded "Don't" in 1958.

   _____

3. Song by Debbie Reynolds (remember Debbie, Eddie, Liz, and Mike?) with a one-word title. Came after "Teddy Bear" in 1957.

   _____

4. The first number-one song by teenage heartthrob Ricky Nelson. The man in the song may have been foolish, but the song was strong enough to supplant "Hard Headed Woman" in 1958.

   _____

5. Everly Brothers song that replaced "Stuck on You" and was simultaneously number one in the United States and Great Britain in 1960. (Hint: Think about a man in love who should be working in the circus.)

   _____

6. Chubby Checker's biggest dance tune. It followed "It's Now or Never" in 1960. (And you thought this was getting difficult!)

   _____

7. Instrumental tune by Les Baxter with a title about poverty in a large foreign city. It was dethroned by "Heartbreak Hotel" in 1956.

   _____

8. While Elvis was "Stuck on You" in 1960, Jim Reeves was trying to convince his girlfriend to tell another man to leave.

   _____

9. Ricky Nelson was in love and feeling youthful in 1962 while Elvis was enjoying the top of the charts with his "Good Luck Charm."

   _____

10. While Elvis was asking for "A Big Hunk o' Love" in 1959, the Drifters were concerned that their woman was drifting away.

_____

11. Elvis was concerned in early 1957 that he was "Too Much" in love, but Pat Boone wanted more love and fewer restrictions.

_____

12. Connie Francis sang about locating male companionship in 1961 while Elvis was pleading for his darling to "Surrender."

_____

13. In the Top Five with "All Shook Up" in April 1957, this Buddy Knox tune about a girl who liked to have a good time was number one the month before.

_____

14. An early 1958 hit by Ricky Nelson that concerned a girl who didn't keep her date. It competed with "Don't."

_____

15. Was popular at the same time as "It's Now or Never" in mid-1960. This song about being lonesome was Roy Orbison's first big hit and one of his best efforts.

_____

16. Pat Boone almost went crazy with this mid-1956 hit that was on the charts with "I Want You, I Need You, I Love You."

_____

17. Bobby Darin got clean in this mid-1958 song, but he couldn't scrub "Hard Headed Woman" from the top spot.

_____

18. This honey of a song by Jimmie Rodgers was in the Top Five with "Jailhouse Rock" in October 1957 and was number one a month earlier.

_____

19. Johnnie Ray went outside and got all wet in late 1956 while Elvis was high and dry with "Love Me Tender."

_____

20. Marty Robbins was glad, not worried, that his big hit was in the Top Five, but not number one, while "Surrender" held the top spot.

_____

⭐ 65 TV and Movie Stars

Several well-known television and movie stars appeared in Elvis movies. Some were already stars when they were in an Elvis movie, but most became famous later in their careers. To make this quiz a little more challenging, there are no names to match or choose from. It's up to you to name the people described below.

1. Made his film debut as a small boy in *It Happened at the World's Fair.* Later appeared in many Walt Disney movies and in 1978 portrayed Elvis in the TV movie *Elvis.*

   _____

2. Starred in *Roustabout* and was the mother in the TV series "Big Valley."

   _____

3. Plays a mystery writer and amateur detective in the TV series "Murder, She Wrote." *Bonus Question:* Which Elvis movie was she in?

   _____

4. Appeared in *Kid Galahad* with Elvis and later in the *Death Wish* movies and other "tough guy" films.

   _____

5. Also appeared in *Kid Galahad* and later became Mary's boss on TV.

   _____

6. Starred as the father in *Kissin' Cousins* and later won an Emmy for his work in the TV series "Chico and the Man."

   _____

7. This actor appeared in *Jailhouse Rock* and starred in many Disney movies, including *The Love Bug* and *That Darn Cat.*

   _____

8. Was the wife of a comedy writer and a Minneapolis newswoman in two highly successful TV series.

   _____

9. Starred in *King Creole* and was in many comedy movies. He was half of *The Odd Couple.*

   _____

10. He starred in *Frankie and Johnny* and in the TV series "Dragnet."

   _____

11. Starred in *Clambake* and in the TV western "Sugarfoot."

_____

12. Starred in *Flaming Star* and played Jeannie in the TV series "I Dream of Jeannie."

_____

13. One of the female stars in *Fun in Acapulco* and in the James Bond movie *Dr. No.*

_____

14. He starred in *Speedway* and frequently had his blood pressure raised by Lucille Ball on "The Lucy Show."

_____

15. Starred in *Frankie and Johnny* and played Elly Mae in "The Beverly Hillbillies."

_____

16. Appeared in *Live a Little, Love a Little* and was one of the major popular singers in the pre–Bing Crosby era.

_____

★ Colonel Tom Parker was the manager for Eddy Arnold, Hank Snow, and Tommy Sands (remember him?) before becoming Elvis's manager in 1956.

Nifty Numbers

This crossword puzzle is somewhat different from the others in this book. Here we are asking for numerical solutions, but you have to spell out each of the answers. Elvis and the Colonel dealt in big numbers. Now it's your turn.

ACROSS

4. On the *Elvis Country* album, Elvis sang short bits of "I Was Born About _____ Years Ago."
5. Elvis's age when he and his parents moved to Memphis
7. Number of second jailbird in *Jailhouse Rock*
8. The number of towns the man in "Kentucky Rain" has been in since he discovered his lover was gone
10. Number of years in Elvis's recording career
14. Priscilla's age when Elvis met her
15. Last two digits of the year in which the movie *Blue Hawaii* was released
16. In "Blue Suede Shoes," it was how many for the show?
18. Number of Elvis Top Forty singles
19. Last two digits of the year in which Elvis graduated from high school
20. Jerry Lee Lewis, Carl Perkins, Johnny Cash, and Elvis were the _____-Dollar Quartet.

DOWN

1. Last two digits of the year when Elvis had his last number-one country single
2. Last digit in the title of the opening instrumental for Elvis's concerts
3. Elvis's age at the time of his death
6. Number of records in the boxed set *Elvis Aron Presley* released in 1980
9. Number of consecutive years that Elvis had a number-one single
11. There were this many Jordanaires
12. Number of years between Elvis's first and last Top Ten pop hit
13. Number of live concert appearances by Elvis from 1962 to 1967
17. The number of the other jailbird in *Jailhouse Rock*

★ "Jailhouse Rock," "Don't Be Cruel," "All Shook Up," and "Teddy Bear" each achieved the number-one position on the pop, country, *and* rhythm & blues charts.

Messages of Faith

Elvis was the King of Rock & Roll, but ironically, all three of his Grammy awards were for religious music. Indeed, some of his very best recordings are gospel songs. (His Hand in Mine is Kent's favorite album.) His religious songs have a more important message than, say, "Hound Dog" or "Jailhouse Rock." Use the message in each song to help unscramble the title of the song.

1. God, I am in awe of your creation and your demonstration of power throughout the universe. Your greatness moves my soul to sing praises to you.

   HUOT AETRG TRA OWH

   _____

2. I spend time alone with the Son of God early in the morning. We communicate with each other and I feel great joy knowing that I belong to Him.

   RADNGE NI EHT

   _____

3. I used to be burdened with guilt, but Jesus placed His hands on me and changed me. Now I'm very joyful and feel like a whole person.

   HUDCOTE EM EH

   _____

4. I was feeling downhearted and weary, but God lifted my burdens. If you have faith in Him, nothing is impossible.

   LEIBVEE LNYO

   _____

5. I'm like a blind man who found his sight. I was very sinful, but thanks to God's grace, I'm not lost anymore.

   CAREG MNGZIAA

   _____

6. I've shed tears of joy because I've found true contentment. I'm happy with God's people, singing praises to the Lord.

   GYRCNI LPHAEC HET NI

   _____

7. Jesus left the beauty of heaven knowing that he would have to die for my sins. Undoubtedly, that is the very definition of love.

   'TNIS EOVL FI ATTH

   _____

8. Jesus knows how I feel and understands my heartaches. He cares about me and supplies my needs.

   TUSJ I EH SOWNK DENE TAWH

   _____

9. Life has many storms, but keep your spirits high. Move ahead and never lose hope, because you won't be taking the journey by yourself.

   KALW REENV ENLOA LUOYL'

   _____

10. Life passes quickly. We may not see each other again until we get to heaven. There flowers will bloom forever and we'll always be together.

    EW RNEVE GINAA TEME FI

    _____

11. Lord, I used to think I didn't need you. But now I'm begging for your assistance.

PEHL EM

_____

12. Lord, if I have hurt anyone or led anyone astray, please forgive me.

RYEARP NA GINNVEE

_____

13. Lord, when I am weary, please stay beside me. Heed my request, lead me through the storms of life, and take me safely home.

DOLR KEAT YM DAHN REIPCSUO

_____

14. Obviously, there is no limit to God's ability. He will receive you with open arms and forgive you, just like He has done for other people.

ON SI RTEECS TI

_____

15. Only God understands the profound mysteries of life and knows what the future holds. But I'm not afraid of the unknown because I trust Him.

OT MHI WNONK LNYO

_____

16. Others may think I'm poor, but I'm not disheartened at all because I'm on my way to heaven. I've got a home in a land where we'll be eternally young and walk on golden streets.

REOV ETH NMASNIO LLITOPH

_____

17. The world is sinful and temptation is stressful. Who else but the Lord could save me and comfort my soul?

I OG DOUCL EREHW OT
EHT TBU ORDL

_____

18. This life is tiring, but I'll press on until the Lord calls me home. Then both people and animals will have a changed nature. Sadness and trouble will be gone, and I'll find peace at last.

NI HET CEPAE YELAVL

_____

19. Who made the forests and the streams? Who made the solar system? Clearly, it was not just a mere human being.

GEBRIG NATH DEBYMOOS
I DAN OUY

_____

20. Why do we only pray to God when we feel lonely or lose hope? Why don't we also thank Him for our blessings when things are going well?

LACL NO MIH EW

_____

21. Without God, I would be a failure and my life would have no meaning. But with Him I have salvation.

MHI TOUHITW

_____

22. You may doubt my words and my feelings, and wonder how I am so sure that God is real. He's holding my hand and that's all the assurance I need.

NI SIH DNAH EMNI

_____

By 1976 (*left*), the costume had changed from 1956 (*right*), when "Don't Be Cruel" ruled the charts.

Books About the King of Rock & Roll

Elvis's life, movies, and music have brought forth scores of books about the King of Rock & Roll. Authors have included former associates, former girlfriends, individuals who claim to have seen, heard, or talked with Elvis since his death, and loyal fans such as ourselves. See if you are able to match the following authors with their writings about the King. Some additional books about Elvis are listed in the Bibliography.

_____ 1. Ed Hill (formerly of the Stamps Quartet) and Don Hill

_____ 2. Priscilla Presley

_____ 3. Jess Stearn and Larry Geller

_____ 4. Roy Carr and Mick Farren

_____ 5. Dee Presley

_____ 6. Elaine Dundy

_____ 7. Red West, Sonny West, and Dave Hebner

_____ 8. Charlie Hodge and Charles Goodman

_____ 9. Ed Parker

_____ 10. Jane and Michael Stern

_____ 11. Jerry Hopkins

_____ 12. Neal Matthews (a former Jordanaire)

_____ 13. Lucy DeBarbin and Dary Matera

_____ 14. Gail Giorgio

_____ 15. Rick Stanley and Michael K. Haynes

_____ 16. Paul Lichter

_____ 17. Steven and Boris Zmijewsky

_____ 18. Lee Cotten

_____ 19. Marian J. Cocke

_____ 20. Vester Presley

A. *Elvis—What Happened?*

B. *Are You Lonesome Tonight? The Untold Story of Elvis Presley's One True Love and the Child He Never Knew*

C. *Elvis and Me*

D. *Inside Elvis*

E. *Elvis and Gladys*

F. *Elvis World*

G. *I Called Him Babe*

H. *Elvis Presley: An Illustrated Record*

I. *A Presley Speaks*

J. *Elvis: A Golden Tribute*

K. *Me 'n Elvis*

L. *Elvis: The Final Years*

M. *Is Elvis Alive?*

N. *The Truth About Elvis*

O. *Elvis, We Love You Tender*

P. *Elvis: The Films and Career of Elvis Presley*

Q. *The Elvis Catalog: Memorabilia, Icons & Collectibles Celebrating the King of Rock & Roll*

R. *Elvis in Hollywood*

S. *The Touch of Two Kings*

T. *Where Is Elvis?*

⭐ 69 New Songs Released Since 1977

Most Elvis songs released since 1977 are rereleases, alternate studio takes, or alternate live versions of previously released songs. However, more than forty new songs have been released! Listed below are twenty of the better or more interesting songs. Match the title and descriptions.

_____ 1. "Alla' En El Rancho Grande"

_____ 2. "Beyond the Reef"

_____ 3. "Blowin' in the Wind"

_____ 4. "Britches"

_____ 5. "Dominick"

_____ 6. "Earth Angel"

_____ 7. "Fool, Fool, Fool"

_____ 8. "I Can't Help It (If I'm Still in Love with You)"

_____ 9. "I'll Never Stand in Your Way"

_____ 10. "Lady Madonna"

_____ 11. "The Lord's Prayer"

_____ 12. "Mona Lisa"

_____ 13. "My Happiness"

_____ 14. "Plantation Rock"

_____ 15. "Signs of the Zodiac"

_____ 16. "Softly, As I Leave You"

_____ 17. "Tweedle Dee"

_____ 18. "Twelfth of Never"

_____ 19. "You Better Run"

_____ 20. "You're the Boss"

A. First song Elvis recorded, in 1953; released in 1997

B. Recorded by Elvis in 1954 on his second trip to the Memphis Recording Service; released in 1980

C. Hit in early 1955 for Georgia Gibbs recorded live by Elvis in late 1954; released in 1984

D. 1951 number-one rhythm & blues hit for the Clovers; recorded by Elvis in 1955; released in 1992

E. Nat King Cole hit recorded by Elvis while in Germany; released in 1983

F. Fifties hit for Penguins; recorded by Elvis while in Germany; released in 1984

G. Hank Williams composition recorded by Elvis in Germany; released in 1997

H. Song cut from *Flaming Star;* released in 1978

I. Song cut from *Girls! Girls! Girls!;* released in 1983

J. Sassy duet with Ann-Margret cut from *Viva Las Vegas;* released in 1991

K. Bob Dylan composition sung by Elvis in a low bass voice in 1966; released in 1997

L. Hawaiian-flavored song recorded in 1966 and released in 1980

M. Sung to a bull in *Stay Away, Joe;* released in 1993, although Elvis hoped it never would be

N. Sung with Marlyn Mason in *The Trouble with Girls;* released in 1995

O. Elvis's 1970 rendition of this Spanish-flavored song proves that he can sing *anything;* released in 1995

P. Beatles song from a 1971 rehearsal; released in 1995

Q. Playful rendering of religious standard from a 1971 jam session; released in 1996

R. From a gospel jam session in 1972; released in 1994

S. Johnny Mathis hit from a 1974 rehearsal; released in 1995

T. Frank Sinatra hit recorded live by Elvis in 1975; a Top Ten country hit in 1978

Bonus Question: The B side of the single "My Way," which peaked in November 1977, was incorrectly listed as "America." What was the correct title?

★ In 1997, the largest-selling artist for RCA Records was—are you ready for this?—Elvis!

★ Elvis first landed on German soil in Bremerhaven on October 1, 1958. During the first four days of October 1998, the city had a celebration commemorating Elvis's stopover. The festivities included nonstop Elvis films, the opening of a music museum, and the unveiling of a plaque where Elvis's ship landed.

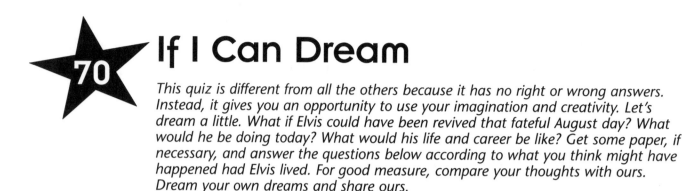

If I Can Dream

This quiz is different from all the others because it has no right or wrong answers. Instead, it gives you an opportunity to use your imagination and creativity. Let's dream a little. What if Elvis could have been revived that fateful August day? What would he be doing today? What would his life and career be like? Get some paper, if necessary, and answer the questions below according to what you think might have happened had Elvis lived. For good measure, compare your thoughts with ours. Dream your own dreams and share ours.

1. At the time of this writing (1999), Elvis would have been sixty-four years old. Describe his health and appearance.

2. Has Elvis remarried? If so, what kind of woman did he marry?

3. What kind of music is Elvis recording and how successful are his records now?

4. Does Elvis still perform in concerts? If so, how often does he perform and what types of music does he sing?

5. Has Elvis starred in any more movies or TV specials?

6. What changes has Elvis made in his life? What special interests does he have?

 Elvis sometimes rented a Memphis amusement park at night. His favorite ride was the bumper cars.

The Ultimate Elvis Quiz Book

Quiz Answers

1. Takin' It Easy with Elvis

1. Blue suede shoes
2. "Don't Be Cruel" b/w "Hound Dog"
3. "Love Me Tender"
4. West Germany
5. Scarves
6. Thomas Parker
7. Pepsi-Cola
8. "Elvis: Aloha from Hawaii"
9. Memphis
10. Priscilla
11. RCA
12. "The Louisiana Hayride"
13. The Jordanaires
14. "Burning Love"
15. "Teddy Bear"
16. Aaron
17. Graceland
18. Memphis
19. Vernon
20. *Lisa Marie*
21. International Hotel/Las Vegas Hilton
22. Elvis Presley Boulevard
23. *Change of Habit*

2. Elvis Is Number One

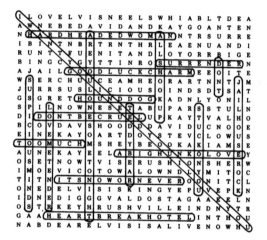

3. Titles and Subtitles

1. "Anyway You Want Me (That's How I Will Be)"
2. "(Let Me Be Your) Teddy Bear"
3. "Don't Be Cruel (to a Heart That's True)"
4. "(Now and Then There's) A Fool Such as I"
5. "It Is No Secret (What God Can Do)"
6. "(You're the) Devil in Disguise"
7. "Without Love (There Is Nothing)"
8. "Release Me (and Let Me Love Again)"
9. "If You Love Me (Let Me Know)"
10. "Long Legged Girl (with the Short Dress On)"
11. "(Marie's the Name) His Latest Flame"
12. "(You're So Square) Baby, I Don't Care"
13. "I'll Hold You in My Heart (Till I Can Hold You in My Arms)"
14. "Santa Bring My Baby Back (to Me)"

4. B Sides of Singles

1. "Heartbreak Hotel"
2. "Ask Me"
3. "Don't Be Cruel"
4. "What'd I Say"
5. "Where Did They Go, Lord"
6. "One Night"
7. "Can't Help Falling in Love"
8. "Stuck on You"
9. "Teddy Bear"
10. "Bossa Nova Baby"
11. "I Feel So Bad"
12. "Love Me Tender"
13. "I've Lost You"
14. "It's Now or Never"

Bonus Question: "Don't Be Cruel" reached number one on the *Billboard* Top One Hundred on August 18, 1956. "Hound Dog" was number two on that date. However, there were three other *Billboard* charts at that time that indicated the popularity of a record. "Hound Dog" reached number one on one of those charts. Therefore, Elvis is credited with a number-one record for "Hound Dog" as well as for "Don't Be Cruel."

5. The Puzzling King

The full name for the item that used only one name is:

15 down: Eddie Rabbitt

6. Not So High, But Great Anyway

1. "Bringing It Back"
2. "Raised on Rock"
3. "Rubberneckin'"
4. "An American Trilogy"
5. "Mama Liked the Roses"
6. "It's Only Love"
7. "Only Believe"
8. "Take Good Care of Her"
9. "For the Heart"
10. "Where Do You Come From"
11. "Let Yourself Go"
12. "It Feels So Right"
13. "You'll Never Walk Alone"
14. "There's Always Me"
15. "For Ol' Times Sake"

7. Identify the Year

1. 1972
2. 1965
3. 1963
4. 1959
5. 1976
6. 1971
7. 1956
8. 1969
9. 1967
10. 1964
11. 1961
12. 1966
13. 1975
14. 1958
15. 1974
16. 1962
17. 1973
18. 1960
19. 1957
20. 1968
21. 1977
22. 1970

8. Where on Earth Was Elvis?

1. Indianapolis
2. Las Vegas
3. Houston
4. Walls, Mississippi
5. Memphis (of course)
6. Beverly Hills, California
7. Huntsville, Alabama
8. Memphis
9. Miami
10. New York City
11. Portland, Maine
12. Toronto

9. Let's Go to the Movies

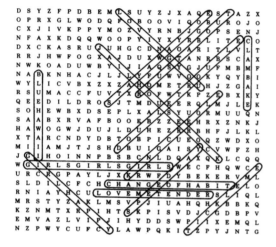

10. A Whole Lotta Blues Goin' On

1. "Blue Suede Shoes"
2. "Mean Woman Blues"
3. "Indescribably Blue"
4. "Something Blue"
5. "Blue Hawaii"
6. "Blue Christmas"
7. "A Mess of Blues"
8. "Blue Moon of Kentucky"
9. "G.I. Blues"
10. "Beach Boy Blues"
11. "Blue Moon"
12. "Moody Blue"
13. "Milkcow Blues Boogie"
14. "When My Blue Moon Turns to Gold Again"
15. "Blue River"
16. "Steamroller Blues"

Bonus Questions: The song is "Blueberry Hill." It is included as a bonus song on the *Loving You* album, and a live recording can be heard on the *Elvis: Recorded Live on Stage in Memphis* album.

11. A Crossword for the King's Movies

The full names for those items that used only one name are:

5 across: Shelley Fabares
14 across: Richard Carlson
1 down: Debra Paget
6 down: Maureen Reagan

12. Second to Elvis

1. F (the Coasters, July 1958)
2. C (the Everly Brothers, July 1957)
3. D (Floyd Cramer, November 1960)
4. B (the Diamonds, April 1957)
5. E (Perry Como, April 1956)
6. A (the Brothers Four, April 1960)

13. In Love with Elvis

1. "Without Love"
2. "If You Love Me (Let Me Know)"
3. "Pledging My Love"
4. "Faded Love"
5. "Ain't That Loving You, Baby"
6. "Burning Love"
7. "I Can't Stop Loving You"
8. "Tonight Is So Right for Love"
9. "You've Lost That Lovin' Feeling"
10. "Please Don't Stop Loving Me"
11. "The Next Step Is Love"
12. "For Lovin' Me"

14. Musical Roots and Influences

1. Jimmie Rodgers
2. B. B. King
3. Arthur Crudup
4. Jake Hess
5. (Willie Mae) "Big Mama" Thornton
6. Dean Martin
7. Hank Snow
8. The Golden Gate Quartet
9. Jackie Wilson
10. Red Foley
11. The Ink Spots
12. Little Junior Parker
13. Jim Reeves
14. Roy Hamilton
15. Bill Monroe
16. Roy Orbison
17. Ernest Tubb
18. Hank Williams
19. Billy Eckstine
20. Roy Brown
21. Rufus Thomas
22. Muddy Waters

15. Top Five Singles

The chronological order of the twenty-four consecutive Top Five hits is:

10. "Heartbreak Hotel" (1956)
12. "I Want You, I Need You, I Love You" (1956)
7. "Don't Be Cruel" (1956)
16. "Love Me Tender" (1956)
23. "Too Much" (1957)
3. "All Shook Up" (1957)
22. "Teddy Bear" (1957)
14. "Jailhouse Rock" (1957)
6. "Don't" (1958)
24. "Wear My Ring Around Your Neck" (1958)
9. "Hard Headed Woman" (1958)
17. "One Night" (1958)

2. "A Fool Such as I" (1959)
1. "A Big Hunk o' Love" (1959)
20. "Stuck on You" (1960)
13. "It's Now or Never" (1960)
4. "Are You Lonesome Tonight?" (1960)
21. "Surrender" (1961)
11. "I Feel So Bad" (1961)
15. "Little Sister" (1961)
5. "Can't Help Falling in Love" (1961)
8. "Good Luck Charm" (1962)
19. "She's Not You" (1962)
18. "Return to Sender" (1962)

Bonus Question: Also reaching the Top Five were the flip side of "Don't Be Cruel" ("Hound Dog"), the flip side of "A Fool Such as I" ("I Need Your Love Tonight"), and the flip side of "Little Sister" ("His Latest Flame").

16. Movie Roles

1. G
2. H
3. P
4. J
5. I

6. N
7. Q
8. C
9. K
10. E

11. F
12. D
13. A
14. L

15. B
16. R
17. O
18. M

Bonus Question: In addition to *Viva Las Vegas,* Elvis also played a race car driver in *Spinout* and *Speedway.*

17. Elvis Covers Songs of Other Artists

Included is the original artist and the year that their version was a hit.

1. Perry Como, 1973
2. Andy Williams, 1958
3. The Pointer Sisters, 1974
4. Glen Campbell, 1967
5. Timi Yuro, 1961
6. Billy Swan, 1974
7. B. J. Thomas, 1970
8. Johnny Tillotson, 1962
9. Ketty Lester, 1962
10. Al Martino, 1967

11. Three Dog Night, 1972
12. Jerry Butler, 1969
13. Tony Joe White, 1969
14. Ocean, 1971
15. Del Shannon, 1961
16. Neil Diamond, 1969
17. Joe South, 1970
18. Ray Peterson, 1959
19. The Bee Gees, 1968
20. Dusty Springfield, 1966

Bonus Question: "Hey Jude," "Something," and "Yesterday." "Get Back" was sometimes used in conjunction with "Little Sister" during Elvis concerts.

18. A Country Elvis

1. "She Thinks I Still Care"
2. "For the Good Times"
3. "Susan When She Tried"
4. "Welcome to My World"
5. "Blue Eyes Crying in the Rain"
6. "Shake a Hand"
7. "Talk About the Good Times"
8. "Padre"
9. "I'm Movin' On"

10. "There Goes My Everything"
11. "You Don't Know Me"
12. "Help Me Make It Through the Night"
13. "Your Cheatin' Heart"
14. "Green, Green Grass of Home"
15. "Why Me Lord"
16. "I Can't Stop Loving You"
17. "Tomorrow Never Comes"
18. "From a Jack to a King"

19. Top Ten Hits

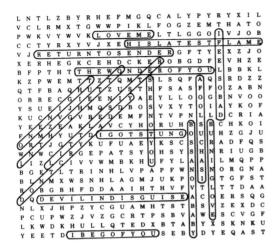

Sixteen of the twenty Elvis songs that made the Top Ten but did not reach number one are shown above. The other four are "Wear My Ring Around Your Neck," "I Need Your Love Tonight," "Can't Help Falling in Love," and "Crying in the Chapel."

20. Ten British Singles

1. "If Every Day Was Like Christmas"
2. "King Creole"
3. "Got a Lot o' Livin' to Do"
4. "Lawdy Miss Clawdy"
5. "The Girl of My Best Friend"
6. "Wooden Heart"
7. "I Just Can't Help Believin'"
8. "Santa Bring My Baby Back"
9. "Tryin' to Get to You"
10. "Party"

Rock Almanac: American and British Top Singles, 1955–73, by Stephen Nugent and Charlie Gillett, was useful in compiling this quiz.

Bonus Question: "Wooden Heart" was a European million-seller.

21. Lots of Plots

1. F
2. L
3. P
4. B
5. G
6. K
7. M
8. O
9. H
10. I
11. E
12. D
13. A
14. C
15. N
16. J

22. Important Elvis Dates

1. January 8, 1935
2. August 16, 1977
3. May 1967
4. February 1968
5. 1973
6. August 1958
7. March 1958
8. July 1954
9. March 1961
10. January 1956
11. April 1955
12. September 1956
13. 1972
14. November 1956
15. July 1969
16. 1981 (a re-release of "Guitar Man")

Total your points, using the point values stated in the quiz, and evaluate yourself with this scale. Including bonus points, there are twenty-eight possible points.

0–5 points:	You flunked. You ain't nothin' but a hound dog.
6–10 points:	Your knowledge of Elvis dates is rather shallow. You didn't love him tender.
11–15 points:	You have a fairly good knowledge of Elvis dates. Find another Elvis fan and pool your information. Then maybe you won't be lonesome tonight.
16–20 points:	You are quite knowledgeable about Elvis dates. Evidently, you have a burning love for Elvis.
21–28 points:	Excellent! You are a true authority on Elvis dates. He was apparently always on your mind.

23. David's Favorites

1. "All Shook Up"
2. "Kentucky Rain"
3. "Just Tell Her Jim Said Hello"
4. "Return to Sender"
5. "Lonely Man"
6. "Jailhouse Rock"
7. "His Latest Flame"
8. "Memories"
9. "It's Now or Never"
10. "Don't Be Cruel"

24. Songs from Movies

1. N
2. O
3. C
4. H
5. F
6. S
7. P
8. L
9. Q
10. B
11. R
12. G
13. I
14. E
15. K
16. A
17. D
18. J
19. M

25. Early Acquaintances of the King

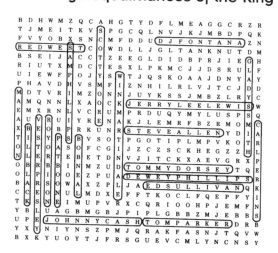

128

26. Descriptive Song Titles

1. "Separate Ways"
2. "Gentle on My Mind"
3. "Double Trouble"
4. "Mystery Train"
5. "Big Boss Man"
6. "Put the Blame on Me"
7. "Little Sister"
8. "Echoes of Love"
9. "First in Line"
10. "Five Sleepy Heads"
11. "There's Gold in the Mountains"
12. "Rags to Riches"
13. "Long Tall Sally"
14. "An American Trilogy"
15. "I'm Counting on You"

27. Songwriting Teams

1. M
2. F
3. H
4. K
5. O
6. B
7. R
8. J
9. L
10. T
11. I
12. P
13. N
14. S
15. A
16. E
17. D
18. G
19. C
20. Q

28. Top Forty Gems

1. "One Broken Heart for Sale"
2. "Big Boss Man"
3. "Easy Question"
4. "I've Lost You"
5. "Don't Ask Me Why"
6. "Playing for Keeps"
7. "Fame and Fortune"
8. "Kentucky Rain"
9. "Promised Land"
10. "My Wish Came True"
11. "Do the Clam"
12. "Anyway You Want Me"
13. "My Baby Left Me"
14. "Tell Me Why"
15. "Where Did They Go, Lord"
16. "Kiss Me Quick"
17. "Clean Up Your Own Back Yard"
18. "Steamroller Blues"
19. "I've Got a Thing About You, Baby"
20. "It Hurts Me"

29. Contemporaries of the 1950s

The full names for those items that used only one name are as follows:

5 across:	Jackie Wilson	11 down:	Carl Dobkins, Jr.
18 across:	Wilbert Harrison	15 down:	Bobby Rydell
6 down:	Ricky Nelson	17 down:	Jerry Lee Lewis

30. Elvis, You're More than a Hound Dog

1. D	6. A	11. J	16. N
2. O	7. B	12. P	17. G
3. I	8. M	13. T	18. K
4. L	9. Q	14. R	19. H
5. C	10. S	15. E	20. F

31. Stories from Elvis

1. O	5. K	9. D	13. L
2. A	6. B	10. G	14. H
3. N	7. J	11. C	15. M
4. E	8. F	12. I	

32. Titles of Gospel Songs

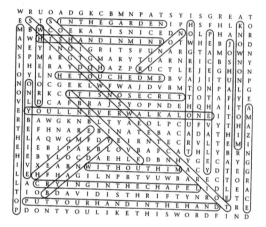

33. Songs from Times Past

1. "Love Me Tender"
2. "It's Now or Never"
3. "Surrender"
4. "Danny Boy"
5. "O Come All Ye Faithful"
6. "Frankie and Johnny"
7. "Can't Help Falling in Love"

34. Name That Album

1. *From Elvis Presley Boulevard, Memphis, Tennessee*
2. *From Elvis in Memphis*
3. *Elvis Presley*
4. *Something for Everybody*
5. *For LP Fans Only*
6. *Elvis for Everyone*
7. *Moody Blue*
8. *Today*
9. *Elvis*
10. *Elvis Is Back*
11. *A Date with Elvis*
12. *Promised Land*
13. *Elvis Now*
14. *Elvis Country*
15. *Pot Luck*
16. *On Stage—February 1970*
17. *Love Letters from Elvis*
18. *Raised on Rock*
19. *Good Times*
20. *That's the Way It Is*

35. Word Pictures

1. "Don't Ask Me Why"
2. "Angel"
3. "Kentucky Rain"
4. "King Creole"
5. "Flaming Star"
6. "Raised on Rock"
7. "Good Luck Charm"
8. "Heartbreak Hotel"
9. "Hi-Heel Sneakers"
10. "Faded Love"
11. "Early Mornin' Rain"
12. "Dark Moon"
13. "The Next Step Is Love"
14. "Love Letters"
15. "All Shook Up"

36. Quotes About Elvis

1. I
2. O (following Elvis's death)
3. M
4. H
5. E
6. F
7. L (as U.N. ambassador)
8. B
9. C
10. J
11. K
12. G
13. N
14. D
15. A

37. On the Country Charts

1. I
2. D
3. P
4. H
5. N
6. Q
7. K
8. C
9. G
10. R
11. B
12. A
13. J
14. E
15. S
16. L
17. O
18. F
19. M

38. To the Movies Again

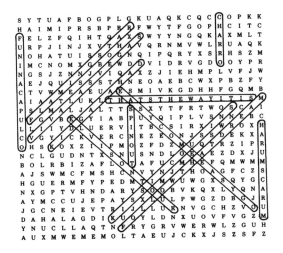

39. More B Sides

1. "Good Luck Charm"
2. "I Really Don't Want to Know"
3. "Are You Lonesome Tonight?"
4. "I Want You, I Need You, I Love You"
5. "Too Much"
6. "Little Sister"
7. "Hard Headed Woman"
8. "Jailhouse Rock"
9. "Kissin' Cousins"
10. "Surrender"
11. "A Fool Such as I"
12. "A Big Hunk o' Love"
13. "Don't"
14. "Wear My Ring Around Your Neck"

40. Elvis and the Army

41. Elvis's Biggest-Selling Hits

1. 2 (double-platinum, 9 weeks at number one, 30 weeks on charts)
2. 4 (double-platinum, 6 weeks, 16 weeks)
3. Not in top ten
4. Not in top ten
5. 9 (platinum, 5 weeks, 20 weeks)
6. 1 (triple-platinum, 11 weeks, 28 weeks)
7. 6 (platinum, 8 weeks, 27 weeks)
8. Not in top ten
9. 8 (platinum, 5 weeks, 20 weeks)
10. 3 (double-platinum, 7 weeks, 27 weeks)
11. 5 (double-platinum, 5 weeks, 23 weeks)
12. Not in top ten
13. 10 (platinum, 4 weeks, 16 weeks)
14. Not in top ten
15. 7 (platinum, 7 weeks, 25 weeks)

42. Loves of His Life

1. D
2. G
3. L
4. K
5. I
6. C
7. A
8. J
9. F
10. M
11. E
12. H
13. B

43. Kent's Favorites

1. "Separate Ways"
2. "If We Never Meet Again"
3. "Twenty Days and Twenty Nights"
4. "A Mess of Blues"
5. "I Gotta Know"
6. "After Loving You"
7. "I Really Don't Want to Know"
8. "Anything That's Part of You"
9. "His Hand in Mine"
10. "No More"

44. Contemporaries of the 1960s

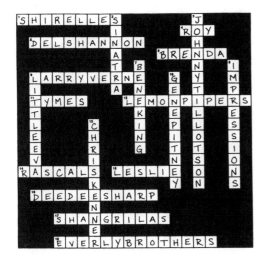

The full names for those items that used only one name are:

4 across: Roy Orbison
6 across: Brenda Lee

15 across: Leslie Gore
2 down: Frank and Nancy Sinatra

45. Dear Elvis

1. "Love Me Tender"
2. "Don't Be Cruel (to a Heart That's True)"
3. "Follow That Dream"
4. "Don't Cry, Daddy"
5. "Return to Sender"

6. "Anyway You Want Me (That's How I Will Be)"
7. "Surrender"
8. "Wear My Ring Around Your Neck"
9. "Treat Me Nice"
10. "A Big Hunk o' Love"

46. Leading Ladies

1. D
2. A
3. C
4. F

5. J
6. L
7. N
8. H

9. B
10. I
11. E
12. K

13. M
14. G
15. O

Bonus Question: Shelley Fabares also starred in *Clambake* and *Spinout*.

47. Money Matters

1. B
2. B (Some sources say $12.95.)
3. C

4. A
5. C
6. B
7. E

8. D
9. C
10. C
11. C

12. B
13. B

48. Number-One Songs by Contemporaries of Elvis

1. "Johnny Angel"
2. "The Three Bells"
3. "Tequila"
4. "Singing the Blues"
5. "The Wayward Wind"
6. "Stay"
7. "My Prayer"
8. "The Theme from *A Summer Place*"
9. "The Purple People Eater"
10. "You Send Me"
11. "Love Letters in the Sand"
12. "I Can't Get Next to You"
13. "Itsy Bitsy Teenie Weenie Yellow Polkadot Bikini"
14. "Blue Moon"
15. "Young Love"
16. "Soldier Boy"
17. "Round and Round"
18. "Pony Time"
19. "Wake Up Little Sister"
20. "Wonderland by Night"

Bonus Question: "Don't Be Cruel" and "Love Me Tender"

49. Elvis Potpourri

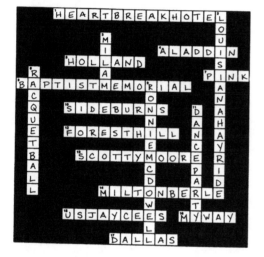

50. Elvis CDs Keep On Comin'

1. O
2. J
3. N
4. M
5. A
6. B
7. I
8. L
9. D
10. K
11. H
12. Q
13. F
14. G
15. R
16. C
17. E
18. P

51. Order on the Tube

A. 8 (May 12, 1960)
B. 6 (January 6, 1957)
C. 4 (June 20, 1956)
D. 5 (July 1, 1956)
E. 1 (March 5, 1955)
F. 10 (January 14, 1973)
G. 9 (December 3, 1968)
H. 3 (April 3, 1956)
I. 2 (January 28, 1956)
J. 7 (January 8, 1959)

52. Elvis Recitations

1. "Are You Lonesome Tonight?"
2. "That's When Your Heartaches Begin"
3. "Green, Green Grass of Home"
4. "Mama Liked the Roses"
5. "Hurt"
6. "Are You Sincere"
7. "I'm Yours"
8. "Polk Salad Annie"
9. "Only the Strong Survive"
10. "Softly, as I Leave You"

53. Perplexing Song Titles

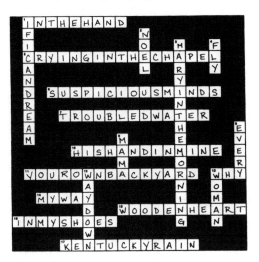

54. Names of Movie Characters

1. H
2. C
3. B
4. K
5. T
6. M
7. S
8. D
9. E
10. F
11. I
12. G
13. N
14. O
15. P
16. Q
17. L
18. A
19. J
20. R

Bonus Question: *Kissin' Cousins*

55. Elvis Dos and Don'ts

1. "Don't Think Twice"
2. "Don't Ask Me Why"
3. "I Really Don't Want to Know"
4. "You Don't Know Me"
5. "Do the Clam"
6. "Don't Be Cruel"
7. "Don't Cry, Daddy"
8. "Please Don't Drag That String Around"
9. "If You Think I Don't Need You"
10. "Doncha' Think It's Time"
11. "Do Not Disturb"
12. "I Don't Care if the Sun Don't Shine"
13. "Don't Leave Me Now"
14. "I Don't Want To"
15. "If You Don't Come Back"
16. "I Don't Wanna Be Tied"
17. "Do the Vega"
18. "You Don't Have to Say You Love Me"
19. "Please Don't Stop Loving Me"
20. "Don't"

56. Backup Groups

1. E
2. J
3. K
4. O
5. M
6. B
7. C
8. G
9. I
10. N
11. F
12. L
13. A
14. H
15. D

57. Incorrect Titles

1. "Little Sister"
2. "I've Lost You"
3. "A Big Hunk o' Love"
4. *Wild in the Country*
5. "Guitar Man"
6. "Kiss Me Quick"
7. "(Such an) Easy Question"
8. *Blue Hawaii*
9. "U.S. Male"
10. "Don't Cry, Daddy"
11. "Kentucky Rain"
12. *Stay Away, Joe*
13. "My Boy"
14. *Kissin' Cousins*
15. "Follow That Dream"
16. "All Shook Up"
17. "A Fool Such as I"
18. *Clambake*
19. "Too Much"
20. "Surrender"

58. Songs Sung, But Not Officially Recorded, by Elvis

1. Q
2. C
3. H
4. F
5. B
6. D
7. M
8. R
9. A
10. P
11. G
12. N
13. I
14. J
15. E
16. S
17. K
18. T
19. O
20. L

59. Friends of the King

1. R
2. B
3. D
4. T
5. N
6. I
7. S
8. J
9. G
10. Q
11. A
12. E
13. P
14. L
15. H
16. O
17. C
18. M
19. F
20. K

60. More Letters to Elvis

1. "Just Tell Her Jim Said Hello"
2. "It's Your Baby, You Rock It"
3. "Patch It Up"
4. "Clean Up Your Own Back Yard"
5. "Take Good Care of Her"
6. "Doncha' Think It's Time"
7. "Make Me Know It"
8. "Baby, Let's Play House"
9. "Just Call Me Lonesome"
10. "Never Say Yes"

61. More Word Pictures

1. "Bridge over Troubled Water"
2. "Burning Love"
3. "Way Down"
4. "Long Legged Girl (with the Short Dress On)"
5. "Blueberry Hill"
6. "One Broken Heart for Sale"
7. "Pieces of My Life"
8. "Puppet on a String"
9. "The Walls Have Ears"
10. "Wooden Heart"
11. "Guitar Man"
12. "Big Boots"
13. "Jailhouse Rock"
14. "U.S. Male"
15. "It's Midnight"

62. Singles and Albums

1. E
2. J
3. A
4. G
5. D
6. C
7. L
8. K
9. I
10. M
11. H
12. B
13. N
14. F
15. P
16. O

63. Contemporaries of the 1970s

The full names for those items that used only one name are:

8 across:	Rod Stewart
13 across:	Barry Manilow
1 down:	Rick Dees

5 down:	Donny Osmond
15 down:	Neil Diamond

64. More Big Hits by Elvis's Contemporaries

1. "Lonely Boy"
2. "At the Hop"
3. "Tammy"
4. "Poor Little Fool"
5. "Cathy's Clown"
6. "The Twist"
7. "Poor People of Paris"
8. "He'll Have to Go"
9. "Young World"
10. "There Goes My Baby"
11. "Don't Forbid Me"
12. "Where the Boys Are"
13. "Party Doll"
14. "Stood Up"
15. "Only the Lonely"
16. "I Almost Lost My Mind"
17. "Splish Splash"
18. "Honeycomb"
19. "Just Walking in the Rain"
20. "Don't Worry"

65. TV and Movie Stars

1. Kurt Russell
2. Barbara Stanwyck
3. Angela Lansbury
4. Charles Bronson
5. Ed Asner
6. Jack Albertson
7. Dean Jones
8. Mary Tyler Moore
9. Walter Matthau
10. Harry Morgan
11. Will Hutchins
12. Barbara Eden
13. Ursula Andress
14. Gale Gordon
15. Donna Douglas
16. Rudy Valee

Bonus Question (part of Question 3): *Blue Hawaii*

66. Nifty Numbers

67. Messages of Faith

1. "How Great Thou Art"
2. "In the Garden"
3. "He Touched Me"
4. "Only Believe"
5. "Amazing Grace"
6. "Crying in the Chapel"
7. "If That Isn't Love"
8. "He Knows Just What I Need"
9. "You'll Never Walk Alone"
10. "If We Never Meet Again"
11. "Help Me"
12. "An Evening Prayer"
13. "Take My Hand, Precious Lord"
14. "It Is No Secret"
15. "Known Only to Him"
16. "Mansion over the Hilltop"
17. "Where Could I Go (but to the Lord)"
18. "Peace in the Valley"
19. "Somebody Bigger Than You and I"
20. "We Call on Him"
21. "Without Him"
22. "His Hand in Mine"

68. Books About the King of Rock & Roll

1. T
2. C
3. N
4. H
5. O
6. E
7. A
8. K
9. D
10. F
11. L
12. J
13. B
14. M
15. S
16. R
17. P
18. Q
19. G
20. I

69. New Songs Released Since 1977

1. O
2. L
3. K
4. H
5. M
6. F
7. D
8. G
9. A
10. P
11. Q
12. E
13. B
14. I
15. N
16. T
17. C
18. S
19. R
20. J

Bonus Question: "America the Beautiful"

70. If I Can Dream

1. Elvis's near-death experience really got his attention, and he has made several changes in his lifestyle. His hair has streaks of gray, but his weight is down to about two hundred pounds and, over-all, he looks good for a man his age. His health is generally good, but he does have to pace himself. His doctors have warned him to take care of himself to avoid possible additional heart problems.

2. Elvis remarried in 1984. His wife, Joyce, a former Miss Mississippi, is twelve years his junior. She grew up in a middle-class home and has achieved success because of her attractiveness and musical talent. She has modeled and made several TV commercials. She has sung with Elvis on a couple of records, but in general she is rather quiet and shuns the limelight.

3. Elvis records at a pace less strenuous than during his early years, but he is more productive than he was in the late seventies. He is careful about song selection, and he especially likes to perform bal-lads and country songs that have already been successful for other artists. He also has a few song-writers that provide new material for him, primarily in the soft-rock vein. He releases one or two albums and three or four singles each year. His songs do not go to the top of the charts but are con-sistently in the Top Forty, or even in the Top Twenty. He has always liked gospel music and is espe-cially proud of his new religious albums. His double album *Majesty and Praise* features background by Andrae Crouch and the Blackwood Brothers, in addition to his old friends the Jordanaires, the Imperials, and the Stamps Quartet. Some of his most recent popular songs include a cover of "I Just Called to Say I Love You," the giant hit by Stevie Wonder; "He Lights Up My Life," a religious ver-sion of the Debby Boone smash "You Light Up My Life"; "Christmas in Dixie," originally recorded by Alabama; and a smoldering new song, "My Love Is a Raging Fire," which is reminiscent of "Burn-ing Love" and proves that Elvis can still rock.

4. Elvis still enjoys doing concerts, but he limits his appearances to about fifty days per year. He does a two-week stint at the Las Vegas Hilton each year, and he has now toured in England and West Ger-many. He had not performed overseas before, and he was a smashing success. His concerts are a mix of pop and rock standards, country tunes, and patriotic songs. In addition to "An American Trilogy," he frequently performs "America the Beautiful" and Neil Diamond's "America" or Lee Greenwood's "God Bless the USA." He places less emphasis on his own earlier hits, but he still does "Don't Be Cruel" and "It's Now or Never," two of his personal favorites.

5. Elvis has had difficulty getting good movie scripts, and he is particular about not wanting to per-form in films that he considers offensive. He has starred in one movie entitled "Triple Trouble," in which he played the distraught father of three strong-willed and rebellious teenagers. In the end, the generation gap is bridged with Dad's music. The film received relatively good reviews (a surprise to many of his critics), but crowds were disappointingly small.

6. Although he does not attend church often, Elvis now says that his search for Jesus has ended and he is an Episcopalian. He has appeared on Robert Schuller's "Hour of Power," and he has assisted with charity telethons for cancer and heart disease. He is no longer surrounded by bodyguards, and his lifestyle is less secluded. He continues to spend several months a year, including the Christmas holidays, in Graceland, but he devotes most of his personal time to his new and spectacular home on the California coast. Elvis has turned his business affairs over to a well-known financial advisory firm that also handles the financial affairs of a number of other entertainers and professional ath-letes. Elvis is very cognizant that our free country has allowed him to fulfill the classic American dream of going from rags to riches, and in a spirit of gratefulness he urges people to buy American.

Bibliography

Bronson, Fred. *The Billboard Book of Number-One Hits*. 3d ed. New York: Billboard Publications, Inc., 1992.

This book, which is updated regularly, has a page devoted to each number-one song since the rock & roll era began with "Rock Around the Clock" in mid-1955. It is filled with interesting tidbits about how the songs originated and how various musicians got together. It also includes biographical facts about the artists.

Doll, Susan. *The Films of Elvis Presley*. Lincolnwood, IL: Publications International, Ltd., 1991.

Provides a brief, but good, overview of Elvis's movies. Contains the plot, songs, and color photos for each movie, as well as behind-the-scenes stories.

Guralnick, Peter. *Last Train to Memphis: The Rise of Elvis Presley. Careless Love: The Unmaking of Elvis Presley*. Boston: Little, Brown, and Co., 1994, 1999.

The critically acclaimed, definitive biography of Elvis, in two volumes. The first book covers the period from his birth until he entered the Army in 1958. The second book is devoted to the rest of his life. Meticulously documented and a must-read for serious Elvis fans.

Jorgensen, Ernst. *Elvis Presley: A Life in Music (The Complete Recording Sessions)*. New York: St. Martin's Press, 1998.

The title really says it all. This book takes Lichter's book (see below) a step further. In addition to giving dates, songs, background singers, and musicians for all recording sessions, it "puts you there" by describing how the songs were selected, the takes necessary to get a master, Elvis's feelings about the songs, and the overall mood of the session. If you buy only four books about Elvis, get this one, *Last Train to Memphis/Careless Love, Elvis: His Life from A to Z* (out of print, but worth trying to get), and of course, *The Ultimate Elvis Quiz Book!*

Lichter, Paul. *The Boy Who Dared to Rock: The Definitive Elvis*. Garden City, NY: Dolphin Books, 1978.

This book chronicles Elvis's life and contains an account of all his recording sessions. In addition, this book is valuable because it contains photos of all regular album and extended play "album" covers and 45 rpm singles' jackets. Chart positions for country and easy-listening charts are also included.

Nugent, Stephen, and Charlie Gillett. *Rock Almanac: American and British Top Singles, 1955–73*. Garden City, NY: Anchor Press/Doubleday, 1978.

Roy, Samuel, and Tom Aspell. *The Essential Elvis*. Nashville: Rutledge Hill Press, 1998.

This book fills a void by evaluating 112 of Elvis's songs that best demonstrate his ability and evolution as an artist. Interspersed among the song reviews is behind-the-scenes commentary that helps to tell Elvis's life story through his music.

Whitburn, Joel. *The Billboard Book of Top 40 Hits*. 6th ed. New York: Billboard Publications, Inc., 1996.

A compilation of all songs from January 1955 to the present that have made it to the Top Forty on *Billboard*'s pop charts, together with the artists who performed them, the dates they charted, and their chart positions. This reasonably priced book is a gold mine of statistical information and a must for all serious pop-music fans. If we were editors of *Consumers Reports,* we would rate this book a "best buy."

Whitburn, Joel. *Top Country Singles: 1944–1993*. Menomonee Falls, WI: Record Research, Inc., 1995.

Another volume by the foremost authority on music-chart data. The title is self-explanatory. This book includes all singles that made a country chart. Beginning in 1973, the weekly "Hot Country Singles" chart was expanded to one hundred entries.

Whitburn, Joel. *Top Pop Singles: 1955–1996*. Menomonee Falls, WI: Record Research, Inc., 1997.

Unlike Whitburn's *Billboard Book of Top 40 Hits,* this book includes all songs that made *Billboard*'s Hot One Hundred, not just the Top Forty.

Worth, Fred L., and Steven D. Tamerius. *Elvis: His Life From A to Z*. Reprint ed. New York: Random House, Inc., 1992.

A comprehensive encyclopedia of Elvis the man and Elvis the performer. Includes detailed information about his movies and all songs that he recorded or performed in concert. A special feature is difficult-to-find information about early TV shows and live appearances.

About the Authors

Kent (*left*) and David (*right*) hope that *The Ultimate Elvis Quiz Book* will be a good luck charm. (*Photo by Pete Bergevin*)

W. Kent Moore was raised with his little sister, Charlotte, on a farm near Ellington, Missouri. Kent's childhood certainly wasn't wild in the country, as he listened to Elvis 45s on his phonograph and the St. Louis Hawks on the radio. He later earned a Ph.D. at the University of Texas at Austin and is currently Associate Dean of the College of Business Administration at Valdosta State University in Valdosta, Georgia. Kent now enjoys being with his latest flame, whose name is Patsy, not Marie.

David L. Scott was raised in Rushville, Indiana, and wanted to become a professional baseball player, a jet pilot, a train engineer, or a newspaper editor. He developed a suspicious mind about these careers and went off to college where he earned a Ph.D. in economics at the University of Arkansas. David now teaches financial management and investments at Valdosta State University, Valdosta, Georgia. David and his wife, Kay, have found fame and fortune as authors of *Guide to the National Park Areas*.